# Summer Sojourn

## *to the*

# Grand Canyon

### *The 1898 Diary of Zella Dysart*

Edited by
Mona Lange McCroskey

HollyBear Press
P. O. Box 4257
Prescott, Arizona

© 1996
HollyBear Press

HollyBear Press
P. O. Box 4257
Prescott, Arizona 86302-4257
(520) 776-4689

ISBN: 0-9651067-0-5

Library of Congress Catalog No. 96-075066

First Edition

*Cover design and illustration by George Fuller.*
*Book design and typesetting by Janet Lovelady.*
*Printed by Graphic Impressions, Prescott, Arizona.*

Grand Canyon scene, c. 1900. *Sharlot Hall Museum Library/ Archives, Prescott, Arizona. (LA 164.1pE.)*

# Illustrations

# *Foreword*

Diaries nearly always make entertaining reading. They somehow take us inside another person, conveying events and ideas that have moved the writer and propelled a life which is, perhaps, quite different from our own. However, we often find ourselves touched with emotions much like our own. This is certainly true of Zella Dysart's absorbing diary. It is doubly interesting. First because it traces an unusual journey, really an adventure by buckboard, to the Grand Canyon, taken by two daughters and two sons of a prominent Phoenix physician. Secondly, and more important, this diary comes to us in its original form, unembellished, succinct, leaving the reader's imagination to flesh out the story and its details.

It was 1898, the end of the nineteenth century, deep in the Victorian Age. A time when most young ladies carefully protected themselves from sun and wind, and young gentlemen were expected to work alongside their fathers during summer's respite. But Arthur, Zella, Winifred, and Fred Dysart, ages 12 to 25, had a summer of adventures. Not only did they ride a wagon (often walking, sometimes pushing!) from Phoenix to the Grand Canyon, but they took the ninety-mile rutted road to visit the Hopi mesas. Zella, 17, recorded it all. Matter-of-factly, as if they were rather common experiences, she describes such unsettling events as sleeping near rattlesnakes and spiders, getting lost in 105-degree heat, running out of water and food, and witnessing the rare and exotic Hopi snake dance. The charm of Zella's diary lies in its unexaggerated, yet vivid, descriptions of a series of unique experiences.

Zella's diary reminds me of Sharlot Hall's early writings. Sharlot, Arizona's territorial historian and poet, wrote of a similar trip to the Hopi reservation in 1891, when she was twenty. Two years later she kept a journal of a wagon and horseback trip from Camp Verde to the Grand Canyon, which covered much of the same terrain the Dysarts experienced on their return from the north country. Sharlot wrote of the same hardships and pleasures, the same landscapes and people along the way. Did these two contemporaries ever meet? We don't know, but can't you imagine Sharlot and Zella, years later, comparing notes on their youthful adventures?

Zella and Sharlot were avid readers and faithful journal and letter writers. Their diaries glow with their acute observations, making us wish we had more of the letters they wrote as well. They each eagerly received letters at unexpected places along the way. Sharlot, camping north of Flagstaff, wrote on July 24, 1893, "My letters were sent out on the stage today. I cannot understand how this happened as I know no one in Flagstaff and had not spoken to the post office people." Five years later, July 30, 1898, Zella wrote, "We are camped in the south suburbs of Prescott. We got here about noon and as soon as we had unloaded most of our baggage at camp ... [we] drove to the city to get some provisions and our mail. We were much pleased to find two good letters from Papa. We read them on the street corner ... "

Both of these daring travelers tucked gentle, sometimes subtle humor into their accounts. Rarely did either of them complain of the cold, thirst, hunger, or fears on such trips. They both gave rare detailed descriptions of the Hopi villages and valuable ethnographic details of the Hopi people and their ceremonials.

They had grown up in Arizona Territory, appreciating its rugged and varied landscapes, making them their own. Unlike many women of their day who longed for the glamour and pace of a New York or a San Francisco, they seemed to recognize and welcome the unusual opportunities which came their way. Zella Dysart and Sharlot Hall would live to experience the enormous changes which would bring Arizona to statehood and into the twentieth century. But in the 1890s they were living their own day and age to the fullest.

Historic photographs enhance this book. Mona Lange McCroskey has collected and included many pictures taken in the 1890s at the places Zella describes in her diary. So it is easy to place Zella and her siblings in the period photographs and to imagine yourself at the age of seventeen or twenty on the extraordinary trip.

Mona Lange McCroskey is a fourth-generation Arizonan. She has earned Bachelor's and Master's degrees in history as well as a Master's degree in Library Science. Moreover, she brings to her task a rich background of historical research and writing, having been published in *Smoke Signal, Journal of the West, The Sharlot Hall Museum Gazette*, and *Cornell H.R.A. Quarterly.* I have relished her "Living History" series in the Sharlot Hall Museum newsletter, *Directions.* These biographical vignettes were drawn from the 150 or so interviews she has conducted as part of the Museum's oral-history program. Best of all, Mona McCroskey combines her love for pioneer Arizona with an untiring capacity for research and a keen appreciation of letters, diaries, and photographs which bring the past to life for us.

"Sojourn." That magical word suggests a brief journey, a temporary stay. "Sojourn" invites us to delve deeply for a while into a curious landscape, a distant time, an unfamiliar land. Somehow it implies a solitary trip, there and back, lingering but not staying too long. So it is with the reading of a diary—a leisurely and transitory glimpse inside another person's life and thoughts. So, dear reader, take this book and your own lively imagination and explore Arizona's deserts and mountains with a quartet of intrepid young people—through the eyes and pen and spirit of Zella Dysart. It's your summer sojourn—or fall, or winter, or spring . . . as you will.

NANCY KIRKPATRICK WRIGHT
Editor,
*Sharlot Herself: Selected*
*Writings of Sharlot Hall*

# Introduction

In August, 1898, four young members of the prominent Samuel Dysart family of Phoenix, Arizona, set out from their home in "Lucern-Croft" on a trip to the Grand Canyon, Flagstaff, and the Hopi mesas in Northern Arizona. They were Fred, 25, and Winifred, 20, both teachers; and Zella, 17, and Arthur 12, students. The sojourners spent seven weeks traveling in a wagon pulled by their team of horses, Victoria and Nellie. Accompanied also by their dog, Trilby, they set out late in the day, to travel as far as possible while the searing desert temperatures were dropping. Fred had made the journey three years earlier, and he repeated his role of driver and guide. Along the way the young people delighted in singing—"a never-failing source of enjoyment to us," and reading—to pass the time on "reading roads," by the light of campfires, or just resting by the wayside. They were avid readers. It was a leisurely trip, and on frequent stops they continued to read, explore, write letters, or simply "lay around." The trip was taken three years before the Santa Fe Railroad reached the Grand Canyon in 1901, twenty years before the establishment of Grand Canyon National Park in 1919, and a year before the Normal School at Flagstaff opened its doors. Campgrounds and tourist camps were few, so the wanderers stopped near stage stations or ranches, or sometimes far from civilization. They remained cheerful in spite of the loss of their precious water in the desert, soaking rains, and primitive, jarring roads through rugged country. Sections of their route later became part of legendary U.S. Route 66,

1

but road signing had not begun in 1898. An occasional board tacked onto a tree gave directions, and in one place a coyote pelt was ornamented with signs!

Zella Dysart's diary entries give us, as well as a travelogue, a glimpse of the Arizona milieu in 1898. Soldiers were training at Whipple Barracks near Prescott for deployment to Cuba and the Spanish-American War. Salt River Valley residents were already seeking relief from the summer heat in the cool pines around Prescott and Flagstaff. The tenor of United States Indian policy in the 1890s is reflected in her description of government housing on the Hopi reservation, already constructed but little used.

The Dysarts visited "The Fields," Frederick W. Volz's trading post along Oraibi Wash between Canyon Diablo and the Hopi village of Oraibi. Volz regularly conducted tours to the snake dances, but these young people chose to make the trip on their own, with a Native American guide. Curious Indians were frequent visitors to the travelers' camp, and friendly Hopis welcomed the outsiders to their villages. The Dysarts watched Hopi dances, were allowed to take photographs, and were even given a tour of a sacred kiva. Earle R. Forrest, noted author and photographer, took the Volz trip in 1906. He recorded his experiences in photographs which here illustrate that part of the journey taken by Zella and her family eight years earlier.

With the help of the diary we can accurately reconstruct the wagon roads from Phoenix to Prescott, from Williams to the Grand Canyon, to Flagstaff and the Hopi Mesas, and back to Phoenix via the old Black Canyon Highway. It is interesting how many friends from the Salt River Valley the wanderers met, that they kept in touch with their parents in Phoenix by mail, and that they encountered a bicyclist. Although some Grand Canyon visitors did make the trip of their own accord before the Santa Fe railroad link was completed, few left written accounts. Most went by stage from Williams, guided by William Wallace Bass, or from Flagstaff, by stage. A seventy-two-mile wagon road built by Bass connected the town of Williams to his camp, established in 1884 on the South Rim west of present-day Grand Canyon Village. Later, Bass moved his operation close to the new Fred Harvey hotel and provided horsedrawn carriages for rim drives. He added an automobile to his fleet in 1914 and competed with the Fred Harvey Company until 1923.[1] Stage service from Flagstaff began in 1885, and from 1892 to 1901 the Santa Fe Railroad operated a permanent, three-times-a-week stage run to the Canyon.[2]

John Hance, a onetime miner of nebulous origin, ensconced himself fifteen miles east of Harvey's El Tovar Lodge, near Grand View Point, where he furnished mules and guided visitors into the Canyon. The first sightseers who came from Flagstaff in the late 1880s found that Hance's camp was the only place offering overnight lodging.[3] Zella described his accommodations: "To be truthful, it is really only a neat little log cabin. Near it are about a dozen clean-looking tents, furnished for rent to tourists." Of Hance himself, Zella Dysart commented, "He is a queer old man, noted for his much talking, and is regarded by all tourists as one of the curiosities of the country." Her characterization corroborates other recollections of Hance, including that of George F. J. Hochderffer. The early Flagstaff civic leader and senator from Coconino County traveled to the Canyon in 1893 and reported:

> *Those who have never traveled over the old stage road to the Grand Canyon and have never seen John Hance at his old lookout will never know what they have missed. . . . John Hance was a humorist. To the tourist he was*

> *part of the Grand Canyon, becoming quite as
> important as the Grand Canyon itself by giv-
> ing an everlasting impression of the wonder-
> ful scenery by his wit and his enthusiastic
> description.*[4]

Miners Pete Berry and Ralph and Miles Cameron, own-
ers of the Grand Canyon Copper Company, likewise shifted
their operations to the tourist trade. In 1892 Berry built the
first hotel at Grand View Point. "It was made of native logs
and was supplemented by tents and the little settlement was
at the head of what Berry called the Grand View Trail."[5]

It cannot be said that these young sojourners were pres-
ervationists: they collected artifacts including arrowheads
and "Aztec pottery" [a common misnomer for prehistoric
Southwest ceramics], antlers, samples of petrified wood, and
rocks from the Grand Canyon. The boys shot rattlesnakes, a
hawk, a coyote, and birds. For food they missed bagging a
deer, but supplemented their diet with squirrel and rabbits.
The diary imparts details about the minutiae of day-to-day
traveling: how they cared for their team, how they cooked
meals and washed their clothes, and how they entertained
themselves. We are privileged to relive the trip through the
eyes of a literate young woman who was "on the trail" by
choice, not as an immigrant or a pioneer. Zella Dysart was
educated at Phoenix [Union] High School, Oberlin College,
and the San Jose, California, Normal School. She taught
school in Arizona at Arlington, Congress, and in the Osborn
District in Phoenix before her marriage in 1908.

The youths obviously appreciated the "slow-moving
[pace that] allowed an absorption and contemplation of the
scenery" and experienced the "growing suspense, an expectation, heightened by the long hours of travel, of what lay at
journey's end, what this Grand Canyon would be like."[6] Ten

photographs accompany the original manuscript, all of which have faded beyond recognition. Nonetheless, Zella's descriptions are so accurate that it has been possible to illustrate the text from archival sources with photographs taken at or about the time of their trip, frequently at the exact location recounted. One has only to refer to Will Barnes' venerable work, *Arizona Place Names*, to begin authenticating stops related in the diary, i.e., Turkey Tanks, "well known water holes in days of wagon travel from Flagstaff to Colorado River points"; and Burro Springs, "on the Hopi reservation. Favorite camping place on road to Hopi villages, makes the Oraibi road feasible for travelers."[7]

Zella, Fred, and Winifred Dysart, c. 1898. *Photo courtesy of John Vaughn.*

Later in their lives, Fred Dysart went into the abstract business in Solomonville, Arizona, and then into ranching in Beaumont and Yucaipa, California. Winifred, after three more years of teaching in Glendale, Arizona, married Ralph Murphy of Phoenix and had a family. Zella taught school for seven years, then married George W. Vaughn and raised her family in Phoenix. Arthur graduated from Phoenix Union High School in the Class of 1904, went on to attend the U.S. Naval Academy at Annapolis, and served as an officer in the Navy, rising to the rank of captain. All are gone now, but they live on in Zella's account. The trip was an experience they recalled with great pleasure.

Arthur Dysart at Annapolis, c. 1904.
*Photo courtesy of John Vaughn.*

Endnotes

1. Stephen G. Maurer, ed. *Grand Canyon by Stage* (Albuquerque, NM: Century Co., 1925), 2. Series of articles about tours conducted by William Wallace Bass.

2. Russell Wahmann. "Grand Canyon Stage Line," *Desert Magazine*, January 1973: 32.

3. Edwin Corle. *The Story of the Grand Canyon* (New York: Duell, Sloan and Pearce, 1946), 207.

4. George Hochderffer. *Flagstaff Whoa! The Autobiography of a Western Pioneer* (Flagstaff, AZ: Museum of Northern Arizona, 1965), 125, 149.

5. Corle, 208-9.

6. Maurer, 1.

7. Will C. Barnes, *Arizona Place Names*. University of Arizona General Bulletin No. 2 (January 1935). Tucson, Arizona: University of Arizona.

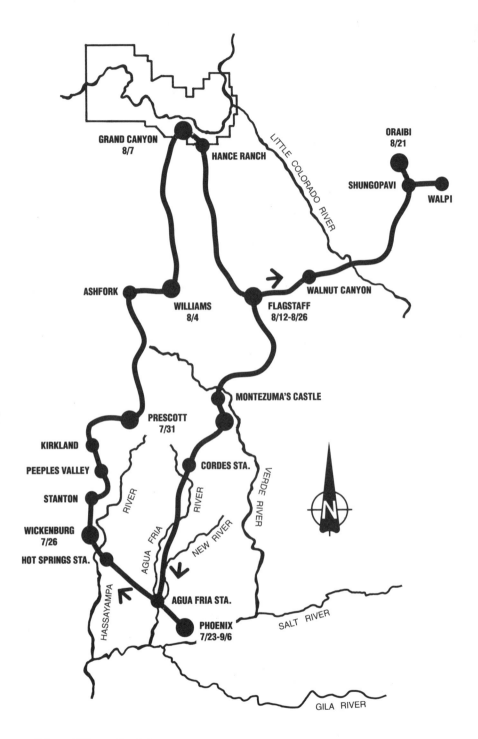

Map of the entire trip.

# Diary

## Saturday, July 23

---

At 4:35 p.m. we left Phoenix for the Grand Canyon. The wagon was packed full. Winifred and I sat perched on a roll of bedding with our feet on boxes, bags, trunks and various other things. Fred and Arthur reclined on sacks of grain just behind the horses. Trilby ran along behind, rather unwillingly. As we jogged along over ruts it was my business to see that a certain bran sack on the water barrel did not fall out. Victoria and her new friend Nell pulled well together. Fred was not feeling well so he sat back on the bags of grain and gave the lines to Arthur.

Winifred and I hung our cowboy hats in the top of the wagon and prepared to make ourselves comfortable. We read aloud *The Village Watch-Tower*. At about 8:30 p.m. we turned on the Betz road about one-half mile from Glendale and camped near the brick kiln. The boys unhitched and we all went with the horses and Trilby to water them at a ditch close by. We unrolled our bedding, washed the dust of Grand Avenue from our features, and lay down. We couldn't sleep much, not only on account of the strangeness of our surroundings, but also because of the mosquitoes and bugs.

## *Sunday, July 24*

---

As we pulled out this morning we got our breakfast from the grub box and ate it. About the middle of the forenoon we arrived at Peoria. Arthur jumped out at the "Green Hut Ranch" to buy some grapes, but failed to get any. We stopped at the railroad station and filled our canteen with good, fresh water.

After leaving Peoria we came to the barren desert and it began to be pretty warm. The road was sandy, with here and there a small hill. Winifred, Arthur and I walked over the sandiest and hilliest part. (I mean always to keep strict account of the time and distances we walk.) We took Trilby out with us to give her a little exercise too, for she had been riding today. The hot sand burnt her feet and made her hop and dance around.

Agua Fria Station in the Agua Fria Valley, 1877.
*Sharlot Hall Museum Library/Archives, Prescott, Arizona.*
*(BU-ST 6006pA.)*

At about eleven o'clock we got to Agua Fria Station. It consists of a Mexican shack where the only inhabitant of the place dwells, the "public house" (if such I may call it) made of a dozen or so posts thatched with brush on top, and the watering place. The well is seventy-five feet deep, with a large water tank beside it. The water is drawn in a barrel by horsepower. The watering place is enclosed by a long rail fence serving for a corral for horses. We stopped near the well and got down from the wagon for a breath of air.

The boys unhitched and the Mexican gentleman came down from his shanty to welcome us. He told us it was thirty miles to Hassayampa and that the only station before there was twenty-seven miles. So Fred said we should have to remain here till early tomorrow morning. The Mexican offered to water and lodge us until then for thirty-five cents, which we thought reasonable. So Winifred and I carried some of our bedding and several books over to the hotel, where the furniture consists of two rustic chairs and a long wooden shelf which we used for table, sofa, and dresser.

After the boys watered and fed the horses we all lay down in our pleasant quarters and rested until we were hungry. Then Arthur and I brought the grub box over from the wagon and spread a luxurious table for dinner. Fred "piled down" and Winifred read in *A Tale of Two Cities.* One advantage of this place is that we get all of the breeze, having no walls to keep it out. But to be sure, the breeze is quite warm—yes, even hot. Winifred and I wore our thick veils to keep some of it out.

The Mexican here keeps a white horse, a black sheep, chickens, goats, and dogs for company. At about five o'clock we went over to the well and watched Francisco, the Mexican, draw several barrels of water with the help of his horse. He told us we should have a hard drive tomorrow, and that three or four horses had famished on the road several days ago. So we will now eat our supper and go to bed in order to get an early start in the cool of the morning.

Desert scene near Wickenburg, c. 1900. *Arizona Historical Society/Tucson, #5328.*

## Monday, July 25

Several times during last night cowboys with horses and teamsters with their teams woke us by coming into the corral, and set Trilby to barking. And once Arthur woke and said something had bitten him on his back in two places, which made him very uncomfortable during the rest of the night. Otherwise we slept in perfect peace and quiet.

This morning Francisco told us of a watering place seven miles away. (If he had told us this yesterday we might have traveled that far instead of lying over all afternoon on the hot desert.) But we started at sunrise this morning with the horses feeling all the livelier for their rest. We passed by the seven-mile station, but didn't stop there. Winifred and I took turns reading our book almost all morning.

At noon we rested in a little patch of desert willows and watered the horses from the barrel. Then we headed northwest, over fairly good roads, with here and there a little hill or sandy spot. It was a pretty hard pull for Vic and Nell, and about 3:30 p.m. when we arrived at the [Castle] Hot Springs watering station they heartily appreciated a cool drink—and so did we, for we had emptied our canteens. We didn't delay long there for we wished to get to the Hassayampa [River], three miles further, before dark.

[Castle] Hot Springs Junction, c. 1900. *Arizona Historical Society/Tucson, #61380.*

The road became very sandy and somewhat hilly. Arthur, Winifred, and I walked some. Fred shot a young jackrabbit for Trilby. About five o'clock we got to a deserted Mexican shanty near the river and camped. After supper we led the horses to the river where there are several small pools of water. But they were too hungry to drink, so we brought them back and fed them. We watched two trains go across the bridge near our camp.

Dark clouds are gathering and we fear it shall rain, but if it should we can make our beds in the shanty. It is a pretty lonely place to camp. Winifred and Arthur have just skinned the rabbit, given part to Trilby, and hung the remainder in a tree for our breakfast.

## Tuesday, July 26

---

We are getting up into the hills now. We have been steadily climbing upward all afternoon. Left camp later than usual this morning because we waited to fry the jackrabbit. It was the first campfire we had made on the trip. We entered Box Canyon and followed northwest along the bed of the [Hassayampa] river. The sand was very heavy and it took a long time to get out of the river bed, which we followed for about three miles.

Shortly after we left camp we saw several gypsies wandering about in a little ravine of the canyon. Winifred read some to us in Dickens. The river which, where we camped last night, had only a few small pools of water in it was now running in a clear stream. We stopped to drink of it, and finding it so good and cool, filled one of the canteens in it.

The tall cliffs on either side of the road made the surroundings look very picturesque. On one bank ran the railroad, and when the river turned west we recognized the spot where the train had stopped several years ago to unload its cars of Sunday School picnickers, at Brill's Ranch. And farther down on the opposite bank we caught a glimpse of the white adobe house through the trees.

We recalled the events of that memorable picnic—how we had drunk of the Hassayampa for the first time and had wondered if [according to legend] it *really would* be impossible for us to tell the truth afterward—and how we had eaten so much ice cream and watermelon.

The road now left the river bed and went over a hill near the ranch. Up and down several small hills we went until we came to one that Fred had been telling us about, upon which on his former trip they had had some trouble in getting the wagon down. So we all got out of the wagon save Fred.

It was rather a steep and rocky descent, and our baggage jolted considerably. We remained behind the wagon in case anything should "drop"—and well we did. For about halfway down, at a slight turn in the road, the trunk (which we had thought roped in quite well in the back of the wagon) came tumbling out, and, striking upon its end, the lid flew open and the contents went rolling down the hill in a promiscuous heap.

Waists, jackets, stockings, handkerchiefs, shaving mug, razor, combs, brushes, shoe blacking, towels—all were scattered in such bewildering confusion that we could only stand still near the spot for a moment to collect our thoughts. Presently Winifred suggested that perhaps we better gather up the things and follow the wagon with the trunk. This we proceeded to do in silence, failing to see the ridiculous side of the accident just then. But, as I write this, seated in the wagon at camp—when the heat and difficulties of the day are over and there is nothing to disturb the calm of my spirit—I pause to laugh, and when I explain to Arthur and Winifred what amuses me, they laugh too at the recollection of the catastrophe.

Well, we carried the trunk to the foot of the hill where Fred had stopped. He looked out with an amused countenance and asked us to "look up the road a little way, he thought something dropped out." Laughing at the joke, we loaded the escaped luggage into the wagon, this time under our feet, a safer but less comfortable arrangement.

We got to Wickenburg at 10:00 a.m. We could notice some increase in the town since we had been there several years ago. We stopped in front of a grocery store and watered the horses at a trough. We also filled our tin cans, barrel, and canteens. Then we drove across the road to the blacksmith shop to get a few bolts put on the wagon.

As the back seat had to be taken out, the blacksmith kindly invited Winifred and me to rest in his shop, which we did. The smith was very communicative, and as he worked, made us acquainted with much of his life's experience and occupation. We learned that his name was Mr. Wisdom and that he had met Papa in Phoenix through Masonic fellowship.

John Wisdom's Blacksmith Shop, Wickenburg, c. 1900. *From the Collection of Desert Caballeros Western Museum, Wickenburg, Arizona.* (P.85.72.3)

Now Fred had been gathering up old shoe leather along the road, thinking that he would try to nail it to the brakes sometime, although he didn't know exactly how to do it. But here was a chance to employ the aid of Wisdom in the job. Ignorance stood by and let Wisdom fix the brakes.

When he was through we drove a short distance out of town and camped for dinner. The sun shone down fiercely and we were glad to get the shade of even a mesquite tree. We laid our table top across two buckets and spread lunch upon it. When Arthur and Fred had finished tending the horses they were very hot. Arthur threw himself down under the tree and heaved a great sigh of fatigue.

Fred noticed the distressed look on his face and said, "Well Artie, we have found that this trip isn't going to be all *sunshine*, haven't we?"

Arthur mopped the sweat from his brow and replied, "Well, I hope not, I tell you!"

After we had packed up, hitched the horses, and written a letter to the folks at home to be mailed at Congress Junction (which Mr. Wisdom had informed us was eleven miles away), we started on for that station. All afternoon we climbed up through the hills and enjoyed the beautiful scenery. We saw many yucca palms [*sic*], which Arthur got out to examine with his natural curiosity.

Soon we turned north upon a rolling plateau. We could look far to the north at Rich Hill, from which (Wisdom had informed us) a Mexican had taken $75,000 worth of gold in one day several years ago, and just west of it the flat top of Yarnell Hill, which is to be the great test of our team.

We intended to get to Congress Junction before camping for the night. Fred thought that tomorrow we should start from there, get to Stanton (which Wisdom had said was seven miles from the Junction), climb Yarnell Hill and get to Peeple's Valley that evening. These were our plans, founded upon the counsel of Wisdom.

But if we had followed the ways of Wisdom in this case our ways would not have been "ways of pleasantness," nor all our paths "paths of peace," for no junction did we come to, and we began to conclude that Wisdom had this time deceived us.

The horses became so tired that they would stop occasionally of their own will to rest. At the foot of every hill we would say, "Surely when we get to the top of the hill we shall see the station." But, the top reached, we would go down again only to see another hill rising its head in front of us.

At last Fred stopped the horses and said we should have to camp here. "There's no necessity in our getting to a station tonight, for we have plenty of water." He unharnessed the horses and went to the back of the wagon to water them from the barrel. "It's a good thing I filled the barrel at Wickenburg," he said. He pulled out the plug, and lo! the barrel was empty! The plug had been loose and our precious water had been sprinkled upon the thirsty desert.

This was very unfortunate, we all agreed, and the only thing to be done was to lead the horses to the Junction, however far that might be. So Winifred, Arthur, and I kept camp while Fred took the horses away. He is still gone now, and we have climbed into the wagon and lit the lantern, which hangs between the two seats just as Papa hung it. Winifred is writing a letter to Stella, and Arthur is watching down the road for the return of Fred and the horses.

We can hear the coyotes howling—we suppose it must be coyotes. It is about the most unearthly screeching we ever heard.

## *Wednesday, July 27*

Fred got back to camp at 9:30 feeling *awful tired*, he said. It was five or six miles to the Junction from our camp, and eighteen miles from Wickenburg to the Junction. We went to bed, wondering how Wisdom could have strayed so far from the truth in directing us.

It was a dreary place—nothing but desert shrubbery to break the monotony of the landscape, and nothing but the wailing of coyotes to break the monotony of the stillness. We soon went to sleep and slept till morning, for there were no mosquitoes and bugs to pester us here.

This morning we drove to the Junction, watered the horses, and mailed our letters. As we were driving out from the Junction we finished *A Tale of Two Cities*. We all enjoyed it very much, but think that perhaps Dickens overdrew the comparison between Frenchmen and Englishmen.

We could now see the mines at Congress at the foot of a

Congress Mine, c. 1900. *Sharlot Hall Museum Library/Archives, Prescott, Arizona. (Item 5, F.4, PB 119.)*

mountain about five miles north of the Junction. From the Junction to where we are camped now there is little but hills, which are quite steep. We turned toward the east and wound around the foothills near Rich Hill. Arthur was brakeman and was kept busy at his job.

Yarnell Hill had been hiding itself behind the nearer hills, but now as we climbed up and turned north near Stanton it reared its head before us and we began to ask Fred how in the world we could ever climb such a steep mountain. He said that was altogether possible, but that we would all have to walk except him. At noon we camped on the commons of Stanton, which is a clean little mining settlement very much like the others we had passed.

We let the horses rest until four o'clock. Although we were under the direct rays of the sun it was not uncomfortably warm here, as it would have been in Phoenix at the same time. On the steep side of Rich Hill, which was now just east of us, we saw white spots which we supposed to be miners' tents.

After we were about one-half mile from Stanton, Winifred, Arthur, Trilby and I got out to walk up and down the hills. All the rest of the afternoon we climbed over the rocky hills. New shrubs now made their appearance—scrub oak, walnut, and manzanita, while prickly pears were almost as thick as the rocks.

Winifred and I were somewhat surprised when Fred soon announced that we were on Yarnell Hill proper. We had expected to see a long stretch of road straight up the rugged peak. But instead we were winding about among what seemed to be only the foothills. The road was very steep in many places, and we and the horses had to stop to rest quite often.

We traveled on in this way, winding farther and farther towards the west side of the top, until we came to the Yarnell

Mine, built right on the side of a mountain. Here we took a long rest, and Fred said we were very near to the top. This was pleasant news to Sister and me, for we thought we never had been so tired. We did not have to climb to the summit of the main part of the [Antelope] peak. We could see that east of us.

Soon we reached Yarnell Station and about one-half mile west of it we camped in a rock glen called Boulder Park. The place certainly deserved its name. All about were great bare rocks shaded by walnut and scrub oak trees—a very picturesque camping spot. We were very tired and even our hard beds felt very comfortable.

Yarnell Gold Mine, c. 1900. *Sharlot Hall Museum Library/Archives, Prescott, Arizona. (M-337pA.)*

## Thursday, July 28

---

The mosquitoes were rank, much to our surprise, and when I woke this morning my countenance was ornamented with welts and one eye was swollen almost shut. Winifred cooked some bread, potatoes, and bacon while I set our little table on a ledge of high rocks.

We were in no hurry to start off this morning, for [the] Bates live only three miles farther, and we intended to stay with them until the next day. So we all "monkeyed around" and Fred wrote an illustrated letter to the home folks. It was nine o'clock when we left the Yarnell post office bound for Peeple's Valley.

At eleven o'clock we were driving through Mr. [C.R.] Bates' cornfield in a pretty little valley that reminded us of Missouri country, and that man with his arms full of corn, yonder, was surely Bates himself.

We stopped and Fred called, "Good morning!" to him. He answered and walked towards the road without recognizing us. But when he did see who we were, his face lit up with a broad smile, and he was so surprised he hardly knew what to say.

When we neared the house he asked us to stay in the wagon a minute, he wanted to "fool Altie." Soon Alta came running out of the house and then stood still in amazement. "Well, of all the people!" she exclaimed, "I didn't expect to see you!"

We went into the house and there was Auntie [Ursula] Bates, equally surprised at seeing us. They treated us so cordially that we felt quite at home and were glad that we had come by way of the valley.

Alta and I were so glad to see each other that for a few

moments we could do nothing but stare and grin—at least that is what Arthur accuses us of doing. We spent a very pleasant afternoon visiting. The weather was cool and pleasant, although Mr. Bates said it was exceptionally warm for the valley weather.

Alta took us girls down to her little retreat in a sand wash where under some large walnut trees we sat and talked. And Alta read to us her latest verses and class song and an interesting story she had written filled with amusing ranch experiences. The time passed very quickly.

Alta and I rode two of their horses to pasture, bareback. Mr. Bates and Arthur armed themselves and went on a hunt. Soon after they left dark clouds began to gather, and about four o'clock it commenced raining.

Alta and I sat out under the west porch while it rained and had a pleasant little chat. Then we enjoyed another installment of Auntie Bates' delicious cooking; and especially her light bread, and good roasting ears just like we used to have in Missouri.

After supper we all sat outside by the front door and talked and sang until the boys were sleepy and went to bed out by our wagon. Alta insisted that it was too early to go to bed yet and persuaded her mother to go with us girls on a serenading tour.

We tramped through the valley about two miles, I think, and serenaded the people at two houses. When we got back we were very tired and sleepy so we made our pallet on the ground and thought we should soon be asleep. But somehow it is always hard for three girls in one bed to go to sleep, and we talked and kept awake until almost midnight.

Next morning we had for breakfast the tender birds killed by the brave hunters. We had been trying to persuade Mr. Bates to rig up his wagon and take Alta and her mother to the [Grand] Canyon with us. They would all have gladly gone if they had thought they could leave the ranch, and Alta kept begging her father to go almost incessantly.

But her mother had not finished Alta's winter sewing yet, and Mr. Bates had some hogs to dispose of and couldn't have been ready to go for a week, which we thought too long a time to wait. So we loaded up and said good-bye to all but Alta, who rode "Old Selam" to the end of the valley with us. Her brother had helped Fred prop up the wagon sheet and build a platform on the back end of the wagon to tie the bedding on. These were two great improvements we had been wishing for.

We had disposed of our lantern at this camp, and it was more comfortable without it jolting about, for we were regretting that we had brought it. At the end of the valley, five miles from Bates', we bid Alta good-bye and journeyed on. We had spent such a pleasant time in the pretty valley that we were sorry to leave it.

We went through the small town of Kirkland and camped for lunch several miles beyond, under some walnut trees where there were the ruins of a house, well, and cave. At night, after riding over hilly roads, we camped near Copper Basin by two tents of an old miner.

After dark he paid us a visit and offered us the use of a tent in case it should rain, which seemed probable. He was quite old, had been in the Territory twenty-five years, and seemed accustomed to his lonely way of living. After he left we could hear him talking to his only companions, his cats and dogs.

We got water at a spring in the rocks. It was so bad that we didn't dare to drink it till [it was] boiled. Arthur thought it tasted like guns had been cleaned in it. It didn't rain and we passed a comfortable night, lying on a mountain with our heads toward the summit.

## Saturday, July 30

---

We are camped in the south suburbs of Prescott. We got here about noon, and as soon as we had unloaded most of our baggage at camp we left Arthur to "keep care" of them, and the rest of us drove to the city to get some provisions and our mail.

We sought the latter first, as might be supposed, and were much pleased to find two good letters from Papa. We read them on the street corner, then drove to the store. While Fred was buying our provisions a rather rough-looking man stepped up to the wagon and asked if we were from Phoenix.

We "fessed up" and he said he was, too, and had just heard that five people had lately been killed by the heat there. He had hoped to get more definite information from us, but having heard nothing of the disaster before, we could offer him no late news in regard to it. When we had made our purchases we returned to camp. Fred says Prescott has grown considerably since he was here three years ago.

The road from Copper Basin to Prescott was very mountainous. We traveled all morning through pine and oak forests. 'Twas a grand sight—the tall, straight pines climbing in stately rows the rugged peaks of the mountains. We could now sing "The Old Mountain Pines" with new spirit.

We are camped in a little hollow. On the hills on each side of us stand houses. To one of these Fred went for water. The lady gave him drinking water, but said her well was low and she couldn't spare water for the horses. So Fred took them to the city for water.

In the afternoon a large, cheerful-looking man came into our camp, said that his name was McElhaney, that he was from Glendale, had come here for his wife's health, was living just over the hill, and were we from Phoenix? We told him our place of residence, name, occupation, etc., and had a very pleasant talk with him. He was very kind and invited us to call in to see his wife and to spend the night with them if it rained.

The clouds looked rather threatening after he left, and we thought some of accepting his invitation. But we improvised a tent with our extra wagon sheet by fastening one side to the top of the wagon and staking the other side to the ground, so we feared neither wind or rain. Mr. McElhaney said it had been threatening rain almost every noon here, but had rained little.

As soon as we were sound asleep the rain began to patter on our canvas roof, and the thunder and lightning were quite threatening. But we didn't get wet.

## Sunday, July 31

Morning broke clear and bright and everything was pleasant, except the flies which gathered about our breakfast table in great swarms. Fred had intended going to church, but we girls thought we were too tough-looking to go with him, so he didn't go.

After lunch we moved a comfort and pillows to the top of the hill and lounged about under the pine trees and read and swang [sic] on a big swing while Arthur was writing a letter. At the summit of a near hill is a large reservoir, which we visited. We found it dry, but were paid for our climb by the good view we got of the town from our elevation.

There are some very pretty houses, some with large verandas with blooming house plants. In fact, there is hardly

Prescott Homes. Martin Home, Prescott, 1895. *Baer Photo. (4059pH)*;
Wells Home, Prescott, c. 1900. *(BU-RE 4052.)*; Kelly Home, Prescott,
c. 1892. *Baer Photo. (BU-RE 4026p.)*; Johnston Home, Prescott, c. 1892.
*Baer Photo. (BU-RE 42.15pB.) Sharlot Hall Museum Library/Archives,
Prescott, Arizona.*

a house that cannot boast at least a few pots of geraniums. This feature of the place, together with the rolling hills, winding, grassy roads, and board sidewalks, gives the town quite an eastern appearance.

As we sauntered back to camp by a roundabout way we wondered how we should occupy our time until morning. Winifred was in favor of packing up and starting on by way of Whipple Barracks.

A storm seemed approaching, but we thought it would probably not rain, at least till night. We were all tired of our camping place and eager to be moving on, so on we went. As we drove through town the wind began to blow and we had to hold tight to our wagon cover to keep it from flapping all over the street.

We stopped at a bakery and I went in to buy twenty-five cents' worth of bread. Fred had bought some yesterday and had been surprised to find it no higher than Phoenix bread. A lame lady with painted cheeks and a great many

Brinkmeyer Bakery, Prescott, c. 1890. *Sharlot Hall Museum Library/ Archives, Prescott, Arizona. (BU-I 178pA.)*

light bangs waited upon me.

I asked for twenty-five cents' worth and she began wrapping three loaves. Thinking she had misunderstood me, I said again that I wanted twenty-five cents' worth, five loaves.

"Three for a quarter, seven for fifty cents, and fifteen for one dollar," she said.

"O! Bread is cheaper than that in Phoenix."

"Yes," she replied. "They sell it at five cents a loaf there. But we can't afford to do that here because we use Kansas flour."

I took the bread and went to the wagon. Fred said he had bought the very same kind of loaves of the very same kind of bread from the very same lady only yesterday for five cents a loaf. Now this is a mystery which none of us have attempted to explain.

It had now begun to rain and men and women were running in all directions, some with umbrellas and some without, some carrying children and some not. There was nothing for us to do now but to drive on until it stopped raining.

So we put on our jackets and coats and held onto the flying curtains. Fred felt chilly so he put on his overcoat and wrapped up in the extra wagon sheet. The rain was fairly pouring down now and we drove very slowly through the muddy streets. I had set my foot upon the edge of the curtain to keep it from blowing out, till my foot became quite wet. I took off my shoe and wrapped my foot up in a pillow to get it warm. This was adventure, I tell you!

When we got to Whipple Barracks (which is in the northeastern end of town) we stopped to consider what to do. Fred was getting cold and wet, and we were afraid he should get sick if he didn't soon get dry. We might go back to where we had camped and impose upon the kindness of Mr. and Mrs. McElhaney, or we might go on and make camp in the rain.

At last we decided to do the latter. We tried to get a glimpse of someone we knew among the soldiers who were hurrying from house to house in the rain, but the curtains of our wagon being down, we could see little. So we drove on, thinking we would camp in the first good, dry place and drive back to the Barracks tomorrow.

Fort Whipple, c. 1900. *Arizona Historical Society/Tucson, #1210.*

About two miles from Prescott we found a good place and proceeded to stake up our wagon sheet in the rain and strong wind. We were finally housed quite comfortably in spite of the storm without, and as soon as we got our damp clothes off and had spread our beds under the canvas, we began to enjoy ourselves.

There were no trees near so Fred was obliged to tie the horses to the wagon, hoping that they were too tired to disturb things.

## Monday, August 1

---

Vic and Nell were very inquisitive about the contents of the wagon and kept us awake some by rattling the frying pan and Dutch oven and bumping their noses against the shotguns, water cans, etc. With this exception we passed a very peaceful night and woke to find the sun shining brightly and doing its best to dry up the mud.

After we had eaten breakfast and loaded up, we drove back to the Barracks. Saw the Phoenix boys ranged in line in front of one of the long quartering houses, Professor Lamson standing before them calling the roll. We were too far away to recognize the faces of any of them.

Fred walked over to find out what he could in regard to the rights of visitors, and particularly, those with heavy wagons. He spoke to several of the soldiers and found from Mr. Crenshaw that we might drive up the hill to the drilling [*sic*] grounds and watch the morning drill.

So we climbed the hill and watched the boys come marching onto the grounds. They had no uniforms yet, but [they] marched well and made a striking appearance. As we sat watching, Lieutenant Will Hill of Phoenix stepped up to the wagon and shook hands with us.

While we were talking with him a little group of about six soldiers came marching up and we recognized the features of Fred Christy. He saw us too as he passed, but couldn't speak until he had gained leave of absence from his officer. Then he came up to see us. It seemed strange for one of our old schoolmates to be a soldier training for the [Spanish-American] war.

We asked him how soldier life was agreeing with him, and he said with his sarcastic smile, "Why, they feed us so highly we are in danger of the gout." He talked rather gloomily, said he didn't expect ever to see Phoenix again but would like to see the Class of '99 graduate next summer.

Soon the call came, "Fall in," and Fred said, "Good-bye, I guess I won't see you anymore," and resumed the march.

Inspection at Fort Whipple, c. 1900. *Arizona Historical Society/Tucson, #23748.*

Mr. Hill told us that at 9:30 there was to be a guard mount, and [he] asked us to stay and see it. We first went uptown to the post office and Artie got a letter from Nat. Fred stopped to see Mr. Ziba Brown at his abstract office. He said there was a road going past Point of Rocks on our way to Jerome Junction. We decided to take this road, as we wanted to visit Point of Rocks.

When we returned to the Barracks the guard mount was almost over, but we got to hear the last of some pretty band music and then took the road for Point of Rocks. When we got to the picnic grounds it was noon and we sat down by a clear little stream to eat lunch. There were high rocks on all sides of us, and along the banks of the rocky stream grew cherries, currants, oak, Johnny jump-ups, etc., vegetation not found in Phoenix.

We washed our dishes in the running stream and swang [sic] in the high picnic swings. Fred could hardly persuade us to leave this picturesque little spot until gathering clouds warned us that we must get out of the lowland. After we crossed the stream several times and got out of the valley we came to a high, open prairie covered with green grass and cattle (which were not green).

Point of Rocks, c. 1900. *Sharlot Hall Museum Library/Archives, Prescott, Arizona. (LA 154.2pA.)*

The broad green expanse was restful to our eyes after having traveled so long over the hills. We went through Jerome Junction, a small mining station on the railroad, and camped by the roadside about two miles beyond, in sight of a ranch. After the horses were loosed Winifred and I rode them to the ranch to water.

An old man was sitting by the well mending a whip. He said it was thirty-one years since he first camped on that spot, where [he] had lived ever since.

[We] went to camp and made our beds. I soon woke with a terrible bellowing in my ears, and by the bright moonlight saw a large white-faced animal coming towards us across the prairie. Fred was awake too, and assured us that there was no danger of being hurt, so we closed our eyes again.

But soon reinforcements came and joined in a weird, unearthly chorus of bellowing. Looking up, we saw cattle scattered all over the prairie, and all seemed to be headed toward us, although they were too frightened to approach us.

## Tuesday, August 2

All night the weird sounds continued. This morning we decided to be in no hurry to start, and to do some letter-writing and other odd jobs about camp. Winifred baked bread for the day, I sewed on the oilcloth which the wind had torn off from the top of the wagon, Fred and Arthur wrote letters to Grandma, Winifred finished a letter to Helen, and we all greased the wagon.

"I don't care if we don't get started until nine o'clock," said Fred. And when at last we were on our way he looked at his watch and exclaimed, "Well, the patience! It is twenty minutes till eleven o'clock!" Then we all laughed and thought it a good joke.

We stopped at several ranches to inquire the way to Ash Fork, but no one seemed to know the road any better than we. All agreed, however, that it was pretty badly washed out. With this comforting assurance we set out to find our own route. Here and there we lost sight of the road altogether and had to guess at our course. Once we wandered a mile or two from our path to water the horses at a stream, and for a while didn't find our way back.

But at last we came into the dim outline of a road and held to it henceforth, for better or for worse (usually worse). We were not at all certain about our road but kept on past arroyo and hill, rock and sand, until sunset. After a last hard pull up a long steep hill covered with loose rocks we stopped the tired horses by a cedar [juniper] tree and made camp.

We were on the summit of a hill and could see higher peaks all around us, covered with cedars and spruce. Arthur made a fire from green cedar boughs, which had a bright flame, and we cooked supper. It was about the dreariest place we have spent the night yet, and our ignorance of where we were and where [we were] going added to the loneliness of the place.

But we were all so tired that we slept comfortably. As one of the party threw herself heavily upon her pallet she said, "O! I forgot that there are no springs under me." "But there are," said Arthur. "There are lots of mineral springs under you."

Hell Canyon between Prescott and Ash Fork, c. 1910. *Mulsfeldt Collection. Sharlot Hall Museum Library/Archives, Prescott, Arizona.*

## Wednesday, August 3

-------------------------------------------

We rose early from our "springs" and were soon started, eager to find out where our dim road would lead us. The road was quite rocky all day. This morning Winifred, Arthur, and I got out to walk and explore the road a little. We gathered spruce gum from the trees, enough to keep us chewing on our whole trip, I think.

I got so warm that I was forced to shed my jacket, which I just before boasted that I could wear all day with comfort. When [we] were tired we climbed into the wagon and jolted over the rocks again. There were many graceful cedar trees about us, and Fred whispered to us to "watch for deer, for it was a gamy-looking place." So we all watched in cautious silence.

As we made a quick turn in the road Fred said in an excited whisper, "There's a deer! See him? Get the gun, Artie!" "O!" we all exclaimed before we saw it. But when we did see it our opinions were divided regarding it. Some thought it was a fawn and others only a large jackrabbit. It might have been either, for it disappeared before we could decide what it was. But [for] adventure's sake we agreed to call it a deer.

Winifred and I finished reading aloud Miss Alcott's A Modern Mephistopheles, and began her A Whisper in the Dark, which we finished this afternoon. We do not like either story very well.

Almost all of the road today was malapai rock (the hardest kind of rock you can imagine), with an occasional little stretch of smooth country. Winifred and I clutched at the wagon bows to hold in while the trunk and grub box crowded themselves around our feet and the tin cans and boxes rattled wildly behind.

We would often come to our senses to find our feet inside the Dutch oven and water buckets and the box of books and [the] long spade tumbling down upon our heads. But we would only laugh and hold on the tighter, reminding ourselves that the jolting was good for our digestion. Fred would look back, and raising his voice above the racket, ask, "Are you coming?" O! It was great fun, I tell you!

About two o'clock we arrived at Ash Fork. It is a prosperous-looking station composed mainly of railroad and hotel, with some building being done. Fred went to a store and bought some candles, canned nectarines, and darning needles, and mailed some letters.

Ash Fork, c. 1890, from postcard. *Sharlot Hall Museum Library/Archives, Prescott, Arizona. (Item 2, F. 3, PB 68.)*

About five o'clock we got to a stream of water. We watered the horses, filled the barrel, got some information about the road from the owner of the ranch, and then jolted on over more malapai rock. As soon as we found a suitable place, we camped.

So here we are, on a little mesa with a good view of the valley below and the mountains around us. Winifred fried some rabbit, cooked potatoes, made some sassafras tea, got out the cracker box—and that was our supper. Then we cleared the malapai away from a small area and made our beds. Winifred and I are now in the wagon writing by candlelight. We are about eighteen miles from Williams, and knowing this we can go to sleep feeling much safer than last night when we didn't know where we were.

## Thursday, August 4

I am sitting on a log by a cheery campfire of oak sticks. We are camped within a stone's throw of the spot where Fred's party camped three years ago—in the suburbs of Williams.

Williams is a busy, rather dirty-looking place. A large lumber yard and sawmills give the town a thrifty, noisy air. West of the city rises the great, green mountain called Bill Williams Peak, [named] in honor of that man who was killed by the Indians. It is the prettiest mountain we had seen because of its greenness and many tall pines.

But going back to where I left us at our last camp, we woke about ten o'clock feeling a few drops of rain and had to perform the very unpleasant duty of rousting ourselves up, putting up our wagon sheet, and dragging the beds under it. It was pretty cold all night, but [it] didn't rain. This morning we started at 7:30, prepared for another day of jolting over malapai rocks. And we were not disappointed. From the time we started until about three miles before Williams we were jolted ceaselessly. Of course we could not read aloud, for it was difficult [even] to hear ourselves sing, so when we were tired of jolting we would walk awhile till we tired of that.

About twelve o'clock we came to greener, smoother country, and the pines appeared again. We had not seen them since leaving Prescott. We had hoped we were past the malapai, but would occasionally strike a rich patch of it to make us appreciate the next stretch of good road.

As we bumped over a heap of sharp rocks Winifred peeped out and said she wondered if she were turned around (we had all been having some trouble in that line). "Which way are we going, driver?" she asked. "

"Mostly up and down and sideways," yelled the driver—and we all agreed with him. Just before we reached Williams the road became smoother, so we resumed our reading in *A Christmas Carol*. It began to rain when we were about a mile from the town, but we drove on without getting wet until the drops began to blow into the front of the wagon, when we had to turn around and stop.

Fred got out and mended the broken brake while we waited. Soon the rain was over and we proceeded, reaching Williams about four o'clock. [We] stopped at the post office and made some purchases at the store, then came to camp in the southern end of town. The trains keep pulling in and out, making a constant buzz.

We have a jolly big campfire which Fred is just replenishing with oak boughs. The fire feels very comfortable, for it is quite cool. We hope it will not rain tonight.

*Friday, August 5*

---

Last night before we went to bed Arthur and I dug holes in the ground by the campfire and put coals in them. In one hole we laid six large potatoes and covered them over with ashes, dirt, and more coals. In the other hole we set the Dutch oven filled with beans, and heaped coals around and on top of it so that this morning we had good roasted potatoes and beans on our bill of fare.

Fred took us to visit the lumber mills this morning. First we went to the sawmill and watched two men riding on a moving saw, which flew back and forth and tore the big pine logs into flat boards very rapidly. The logs came whizzing into the mill upon a car, great levers caught them, and after the men on the saw had made rough boards of them, more men and machinery caught them and cut the rough edges off. Then they were loaded into cars and taken to the dry kiln, which we next visited.

Saginaw & Manastee Lumber Co., Williams, c. 1900.
*Arizona Historical Society/Pioneer Museum,*
*Flagstaff. NAPHS #7-7.*

The boss there showed us a hot room in which was piled the lumber to be dried. He told us to put our heads in at the door. We did so, and the hot air coming from the room reminded us of Phoenix at noon. At the planing mill we saw the dried lumber being sent through great rollers, from which it came out, smooth and slick, to be stacked in the lumberyard or made into boxes.

From the mills we went by the post office. [We] saw Mr. Altenburg, who had come from Phoenix on his bicycle in four days, a distance of 244 miles.

Upon reaching camp Winifred and I began washing with all our might. By noon we had quite a respectable-looking line of clothes hanging on the hill and were eating our dinner in the tent with extreme satisfaction. As soon as our clothes had dried we began loading up and at four o'clock were started from Williams.

A calamity happened to us just now—our bale of hay got loose and was threatening to blow away. Having corralled it as best we could, we drove on, ceaselessly bumping over malapai until dusk. Before we camped it rained hard, and was so cold that all the wraps obtainable were comfortable.

When the rain had ceased we hoisted our tent, built a roaring fire of fallen spruce boughs, and warmed ourselves. We set the table by the fire, Winifred mixed some batter, and Fred delighted in flapping the cakes in the frying pan, an accomplishment he had learned on his former camping trip.

## Saturday, August 6

We rode today over much the same kind of country as we did yesterday—rolling prairie, with here and there a cluster of spruce and cedar trees, and sagebrush, grass and malapai rocks in abundance.

Once we saw some timid antelope in the distance, and again we saw a yellow animal about the size of Trilby, the identity of which we could not determine.

"It is about the size of a badger," said Arthur.

"I believe it is a wildcat," said Fred.

"Don't you think it might be a mountain lion?" suggested Winifred.

"No," I said, "it is only a coyote."

As a compromise we decided to coin a name for the creature which would satisfy us all. So we named it a "badg-cat-ion-oyte."

We made camp among the spruce and cedar trees and now have a jolly big campfire, by which I am sitting upon a log.

## Sunday, August 7

This morning we breakfasted upon hotcakes, butter, and honey. Someone remarked this morning that next winter when we are busy teaching school, keeping books, and learning lessons we shall look back upon our summer outing with pleasant memories and long in vain to spend such another morning as this. So we resolved to get all the enjoyment possible during our trip (a resolution scarcely necessary).

Arthur shot a large hawk that had been hovering about our camp this morning. We started off in high spirits, bound for the Grand Canyon, our journey's destination. All morning we traveled over beautiful, smooth country, but towards noon our route led through a hollow, and then through a winding canyon.

At two o'clock we reached Rain Tanks, where we watered the horses. From here we took our road to the Canyon, through pine, spruce, and cedar forests, and we "children" gathered some spruce gum.

The trees were so thick that had the Canyon been just in front of us we could not have seen it. But Fred had told us that we should approach it on level country and should not see it until we were on its brink, so we were expecting to be surprised in that way.

The "children" became somewhat impatient and ran ahead of the wagon, each eager to be the first to see the grand sight. Indeed, Winifred became so excited that she stopped her search under a cedar tree for spruce gum.

After we girls had become tired and had returned to the wagon, a glad shout from Arthur, who had disappeared through the trees, proclaimed that the Canyon was near us. Yes! through the dense forest we could soon see a wide blue band resting upon the ground—the walls of the great [Grand] Canyon.

We girls scrambled out eagerly to behold the grand sight—and such a sight it was! Down, down we looked over great strata of rock looking like ancient temples of the gods, each a mountain in itself, so tall, so blue and so majestic. Down! down 5,000 feet or more to where the muddy Colo-

View of Grand Canyon from Rowe's Point, 1905. *Sharlot Hall Museum Library Archives, Prescott, Arizona. (LA206dd.)*

rado [River] threads in its course, so far away that we could neither hear nor see the rushing of its mighty waters.

Through the deep gorges of both walls numerous tributaries flowed, winding their ways among the rocky ledges. The view was quite extensive but very much of the same— great flat mountains forming an immense stairway that scaled the rugged walls of the great gorge. All was blue save for the golden tints left by the setting sun.

When we had given utterance to our first raptures, we drove back into the forest to find a camping place for the night. About a quarter of a mile from the rim of the Canyon the boys unhitched and tied the horses. Then we all walked back to take another look before going to bed.

When we had returned to camp we spread out the beds amid the thickly growing trees. It was quite a lonely place. Winifred was afraid a badgcationoyte would come into camp and devour us all; so Fred loaded the shotgun and placed it in her reach. He and Arthur slept with the rifle and revolver at their heads, and brave Trilby was my defense.

## Monday, August 8

We went back to Rowe's Well and there took a road leading to "The Indian Garden Trail," which we reached at noon. Winifred, Arthur, and I walked down about one-half mile just to see what a mountain trail was like.

We soon satisfied our curiosity and didn't care to go farther. The path was so very winding that in traveling one-half mile we had gone perpendicularly only a very short distance. On this little walk we saw for the first time some genuine hemlock trees.

After we climbed back to the wagon we drove to Rain Tanks and watered the horses. Fred wished us to see the

Rowe's Well near Grand Canyon, c. 1900. *C.H. Shaw Photo. Sharlot Hall Museum Library/Archives, Prescott, Arizona. (PO 555pb.)*

Canyon from the Hance trail, so we took a road going in that direction which Fred thought would probably lead into the main road from Flagstaff to the Hance trail. We traveled through the most restful-looking and pleasant country we have yet seen.

Green, rolling hills, dense woods of tall pines and shaggy oaks; yellow, bright-eyed daisies, deep red "Indian paint" flowers, larkspur and other varieties of wild blossoms—each added its peculiar beauty and helped to make a landscape faultless in beauty.

We hoped to find the main Flagstaff road before camping, and that is why we rode and rode long after dark. Arthur and I took turns reading aloud *The Chimes,* and when it had grown too dark for this we amused ourselves by singing—a never-failing source of enjoyment to us.

We discovered two pairs of antlers hanging upon a pine tree near the road. Of course we put them in the wagon to take home as souvenirs. About nine o'clock Fred concluded we had better go no farther, as the road was rough and little

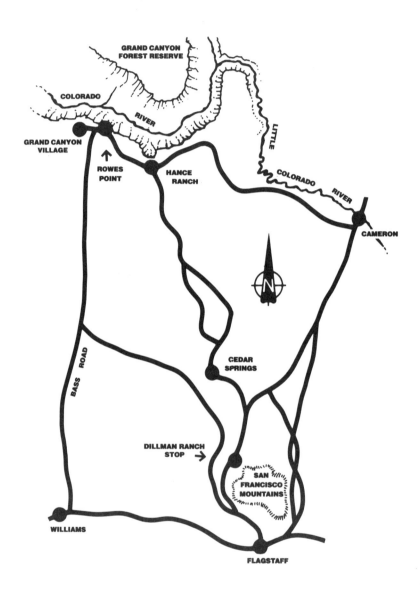

Map of stage routes from Williams and Flagstaff to the Grand Canyon.

traveled and the night was dark.

Arthur started a bright fire with dry pine cones and needles, and we set up our tent. We all agreed that this camping place exceeded all our others in wildness. Gathering clouds and flashes of lightning foretold a storm, and we shuddered to think of sleeping near the tall pines, exposed to the fierce elements.

## Tuesday, August 9

But no storm came. Morning found us up and on our way. Fred had remarked last night that we would probably be surprised this morning to find how near we were to the main road when we camped. And sure enough! We had traveled no more than a mile before we came to the well-traveled Flagstaff road.

We met the United States Mail Stage on its way to Flagstaff, a trip which it makes every second day. Both of the passengers were strangers to us. We came to a fork in the road, one branch leading to Cameron and the other to the Hance trail. Upon the signboard that told us this were the signatures of Ross Crouse and Ross Russell, whose party had left Phoenix a week before us.

About noon we arrived at the Hance trail. Now the Hance Hotel at this place is not so large or so grand as the Adams or Ford [Hotels] of Phoenix. To be truthful, it is really only a neat little log cabin. Near it are about a dozen clean-looking tents, furnished for rent to tourists. Business is centered in a small cabin in which is post office and store. We got out of the wagon and walked over to the board fence where stood a young man. He asked us to come in and put up at the hotel. We walked inside the fence and sat down upon a wooden bench by a cage of pine squirrels. While the rest of us were watching the frolickings of these pretty creatures, Fred and the strange young man were engaged in conversation. Fred told our name and asked if any parties had been there from Phoenix lately. The man said yes, but he didn't remember any of their names.

He had met Father in Phoenix about a year ago and had known him before that in Lancaster, Missouri, and also in Memphis, where he himself had once lived.

"Indeed!" said Fred.

"Yes, my name is Simington. I left Missouri four years ago."

"And I also about that time."

"Were you the young man who left Lancaster for his health?" asked Mr. Simington.

"That was my case exactly," answered Fred.

"Well, then I have a message for you. A young lady in Lancaster—a Miss Jewett, told me the night I left that if I ever saw you to tell you 'Hello' for her."

Now this was strange, that Fred should meet someone in this lonely place who four years ago had left our home town charged with a message to him.

We climbed a little hill back of the hotel and viewed the Canyon once more from Lookout Rock. We each carried away a piece of the rock for a souvenir. Then we returned to the wagon and drove to the "camping grounds," which differ from the other land of the great Coconino Forest only in having pastures fenced in for stock, a pond of water, and four log houses. Of these conveniences we are making use of but one, i.e., the water. We preferred to camp in the open forest and let our horses run loose.

So here we are, then! Fred has just recovered from a nap, and he and Arthur are getting their guns ready for a hunt. Winifred and I have been washing our hair and are

John Hance at his Camp, November 16, 1895. *Sharlot Hall Museum Library/Archives, Prescott, Arizona. (PO 1705p.)*

John Hance's Camp, c. 1900. *Arizona Historical Society/Pioneer Museum, Flagstaff. NAPHS #340-10.*

letting it dry while we write. The water here is nice and soft, but unfit to drink. Drinking water is hauled from Cedar Springs, forty miles away. Tomorrow morning we will start for Cedar Springs. We are eager to get to Flagstaff and get our mail from home.

## Wednesday, August 10

Yesterday p.m. I roamed through the pine woods near our camp and gathered wild flowers—just like we used to do "in the U.S."

I came across Fred and Arthur on their hunt. Arthur insisted that I should shoot the rifle, which I at last consented to do. So he explained in detail the workings of the different parts of the gun, and instructed me how to manipulate them. My target was to be the center of the end of a pine log.

All was ready but the pulling of the trigger. Could I do it? What if the awful weapon should whirl round and strike me or Arthur! But that was very improbable, and besides I must not allow Arthur to perceive that I was at all afraid. So I excused my hesitancy by forgetting "*just* how you told me to pull the trigger."

When I had been reinstructed in regard to this, I again took steady aim, placed my finger upon the fatal trigger, screwed my courage to its highest pitch—and actually fired! How proud I felt to know that I had caused the forests to reverberate [as] loudly as any brave hunter—I who had never shot a weapon before. And Arthur was considerate enough of my feelings to praise my bravery and express his surprise that I could have hit so near the mark (I struck the log about a foot from the center).

While we were cooking supper a light wagon with five men drove up. They inquired of us where they were and made camp near us. We watched them build their fire and set up their tent, and remarked to each other that they were surely fresh from the east, else they would prefer to sleep under the vaulted heavens.

Wishing to show his friendliness, fellow feeling, etc., Fred went to their camp and asked pleasantly of one of them who was pounding the stakes of the tent, "Where are you from?"

"Flag," gruffly muttered the man without looking up—and Fred ventured his next remark to another of the party. He soon returned and reported our neighbors to be an unsociable set.

But while we were sitting comfortably around our campfire and Arthur was reading *The Chimes* to us by candlelight, one of the men, more sociably inclined than the others, came to our camp, and sitting upon our cracker box (which we reserve for guests) talked pleasantly, telling us about himself and [his] companions. They were lumbermen from Flagstaff and were having a "layoff" on account of the great catastrophe that had happened to the lumber mills there last week. A great fire had destroyed the mills and caused a loss of $75,000.

This morning we got an early start, not waiting for even our breakfast. A draft of hot tea, made upon a quick fire of pine cones and hastily drunk before we started, satisfied us until we could get to smooth roads and safely pull out the grub box.

But I must mention the fact that before we left camp we saw and talked with Mr. Hance, the owner and boss of the plantation. He is a queer old man, noted for his much talking, and is regarded by all tourists as one of the curiosities of the country. He spends part of his time escorting tourists

# The Flagstaff Gem

FLAGSTAFF, ARIZONA, THURSDAY, AUGUST 4, 1898

## A DISASTROUS FIRE IN MILTON

### THE ARIZONA LUMBER & TIMBER CO'S. MILLS DESTROYED.

## LOSS, ABOUT $50,000

Tuesday afternoon about 3 o'clock it was discovered that the Arizona Lumber & Timber Co's. saw mill, planing mill and box factory was on fire and the alarm was immediately given. The fire company with their engine, and almost the entire population of Flagstaff went to the scene of the fire as quickly as they could make a mile (It being that distance from the business part of town) and rendered all the assistance within human power to save this valuable property, but it was an impossibility . . . .

The Arizona Lumber & Timber Co. has been foremost in all of Flagstaff's enterprises and gave employment to a large number of men at good wages, and their misfortune is heavily felt here. One thing can truly be said to their credit as a corporation that they have not been oppressive or tried to beat their employees out of a cent; . . . .

Newspaper article from *The Flagstaff Gem,* August 4, 1898.

down his trail to the bottom of the Canyon and keeps mules for that express purpose, charging five dollars apiece for the trip.

We started toward Flagstaff, intending to reach Cedar Springs by night. At noon we stopped under some spruce trees and ate dinner. Fred watered the horses from the barrel and let them graze for about an hour. Then I read to him till he fell asleep upon a quilt on the ground.

Meanwhile Winifred and Arthur were gathering spruce gum, thinking it would be the last chance. After we first started we traveled over a few hills, and then came to an open prairie. San Francisco Peak reared its great blue head in the southwest, and just west of it we thought we saw Bill Williams Mountain.

About six o'clock we arrived at Cedar Springs. The spring and house are on the slope of a hill, luxuriant in malapai rock. The water comes through an iron pipe, in a cold pure stream, and empties into a series of troughs arranged each higher than the next below it.

Cedar Springs, en route to Grand Canyon, 1898. #74.1984, *Fred Clatworthy Collection, Museum of Northern Arizona.*

We drove by the house and barn and are camped upon the side of the hill, east of them. The water and air is [*sic*] excellent, and if we can scrape enough rocks away to make our beds, we shall pass a very comfortable night.

## Thursday, August 11

---

We are camped in *still* the prettiest place. The road from Cedar Springs was at first hilly, with many cedar trees. When we were about a mile from the springs we hitched the horses to a tree and climbed a steep little hill to where Fred said the petrified wood grew. We didn't find it in large, living trees, however, as one might expect, but only in chunks and chips lying on the sides of the hill.

We spent an hour or two hunting petrified wood and returned to the wagon with our pockets and arms full of specimens. Before we had traveled far Fred said in a very subdued voice, "Well, sir, I saw either a deer or a burro go behind that cedar tree. Whoa!" A moment of silent watching.

Then a slender form appeared from behind the tree about one hundred yards away. Another behind it! Yes, they were deer! Then another and another! until we had counted five grown deer, and behind them two small ones. Seven deer, and within shot! This was beyond our greatest expectation. Quickly Fred gave me the lines, seized the shot-gun, loaded it, and was just aiming at the innocent heads when cautious Vic, suspecting what was going on, thought it time for her to begin to back and prance around.

This scared the deer (who until then had been unaware of our presence) and put them immediately to flight just as the shot was fired in among them. Although Fred leaped out and swiftly ran after them, he saw them no more. They had sped far o'er the hills and were hidden by the trees.

We were all so excited over the adventure and so thankful for having seen so many deer together that we forgot to be disappointed in not shooting a single one. Fred declared, however, that he intended to give Vic a good whipping the next time she behaved so, which time, alas for the poor horse! was soon to come.

For, after dinner when we had come into the region of grass and tall pines, Fred saw a pine squirrel which he thought would be very delicious for our supper. So Trilby was sent to tree it, and Fred ran to shoot it. As soon as the wagon had stopped Vic guessed that there was to be shooting and began to prance and back downhill, so that it was all Winifred and I could do to keep her from turning us over. But after the squirrel had fallen dead, Vic received her promised and much-deserved punishment.

Soon we began to climb the hills—the low foothills of San Francisco Peak which lies southeast of us. Silvery quaken [sic] aspen trees made their appearance and arranged themselves in belts and groves around the green hills.

We reached Little Springs about three o'clock and are camped about one-half mile south, in a little grove of quaken aspens, hemlocks, and pines—such a beautiful place. The hills are covered with tall ripe grass so that the horses are bewildered and don't know where to begin grazing. Various kinds of pretty wild flowers grow thick in the long grass.

Winifred is making a squirrel pot pie. We will set our table on some boulders under a hemlock tree on the slope of the hill. We passed by *acres* of ferns just before we camped. They are of a large, coarse variety, but very pretty. There is a large patch of them near our camp. This is by far the prettiest little glen we have camped in yet, and I will regret to leave it.

O, yes! About two miles from Little Springs we met

two camping wagons and in one were Katie Smith, her father and mother, of Phoenix, on their way to the Canyon.

En route to Grand Canyon from San Francisco Peaks, 1903. *#74.1986, Fred Clatworthy Collection, Museum of Northern Arizona.*

Buckboard en route to Grand Canyon from San Francisco Peaks, 1903. *#74.1985, Fred Clatworthy Collection, Museum of Northern Arizona.*

# Friday, August 12

---

We are in camp at the foot of Observatory Hill in the west end of Flagstaff, having arrived here at three o'clock this p.m. We were very pleased to find nine newsy letters waiting for us. Mr. Hugh Evans of Phoenix visited us this afternoon. He is en route to California.

It rained this afternoon and still looks cloudy. We intended to visit the Observatory this evening, but on account of the stormy appearance of the sky [we] gave it up, much to the disappointment of Arthur.

View of Flagstaff and dome of 24-inch telescope at Lowell Observatory, c. 1900. *Arizona Historical Society/Pioneer Museum, Flagstaff. NAPHS #349.3.*

## Saturday, August 13

---

Winifred and I washed some clothes this a.m. After dinner Mr. Plank came to see us. When he had gone Winifred and I "strake off" to find some Phoenix people. We first called on Nellie Persons and her mother from Phoenix, who have been here about a week. Nellie took us to see Miss McCowan.

## Sunday, August 14

---

Miss McCowan, Nellie, her mother, and Minnie Hill came to see us last evening. Miss McCowan persuaded us to go to the Moqui [Hopi] Indian Reservation about ninety miles northeast from here, and take her. She saw Mr. Reed, who has once been to the reservation, and he gave us full directions as to the road.

We shall probably start tomorrow at noon. Winifred and I called upon Mrs. Miller this morning. Winifred had met her in Phoenix. She was sick abed, but very sweet and sociable notwithstanding. There are two other camping outfits near us.

We find many varieties of flowers, and take long tramps over the hills through the thickly growing goldenrod and daisies.

## Monday, August 15

Mr. and Mrs. Plank called yesterday afternoon. This morning we loaded our things in the wagons and drove to Mr. Olney's house, where Miss McCowan lives. Mr. Olney was kind enough to let us stow some of our plunder in his barn so that we should have room for another passenger. Fred met Mr. Reed and received a diagram of the road and parting instructions from him.

Mr. Poyen came to our camp this morning and asked us to carry supplies for him so that he could go with us on his pony. But we had to refuse. So he arranged for a buck-board and team, and he and his wife will both go with us.

After we got Miss McCowan we rode by the house where they are stopping. They were not yet ready and asked us to wait for them. We waited about a half hour and then drove on, promising to wait again at the fork of the road seven miles further.

We are now stopped at the seven-mile fork and Fred has walked back to meet Mr. and Mrs. Poyen. Arthur is holding the team. Winifred is roaming through the woods, and "Teacher" and I are reclining upon a pile of large stones by the roadside eating crackers and writing diaries.

Mr. Reed lent us some books describing the customs and ceremonials of the Hopi Indians. We read some in them on the way from Flagstaff.

## Tuesday, August 16

---

Mr. and Mrs. Poyen overtook us and we resumed our journey. In spite of Mr. Reed's particular instructions, at every forking of the road we felt a little dubious and caught ourselves making several mistakes.

Once our road led us to a lumber camp by the railroad. This was mistake number one, and we regretted it more on account of our followers than for our own sakes, for now their faith in us would be shaken. We thought now that we could at least show some cleverness in finding our lost road again, so we cut across the country over brush and rocks, where perhaps no other wagon had ever been pulled.

The first road we came to we followed until we were inwardly much disappointed to find it approach[ed] the railroad. We knew then that, according to Mr. Reed's directions, it could not be the right road. I say we were disappointed inwardly. We took care to show no anxiety upon our faces when we spoke to our friends in the rear, for Mr. Poyen was already becoming as fretful and worried as a little child. (He is naturally of a nervous disposition.)

With fear and trembling we began to wander about again in search of another road. We soon found one going in a suitable direction. As we took it, Fred called assuringly to our friends in the rear, "Here we are!" They seemed satisfied for awhile. Mrs. Poyen hugged her dog closer to her and Mr. Poyen smoked his pipe in silence.

We began to feel easier and had just commenced reading again about the Indians, when—O woe unutterable! We were again approaching the railroad. "Well, we're not on the right road yet," said Fred.

"And the worst thing about it is that 'our friends in the

rear' will know it," laughed Miss McCowan. "What if they should take a notion to go back to Flagstaff! Of course they would tell all the people that we had taken them out amongst the pines and lost them." O dear! O dear! Such a time we are having.

As the road seemed pretty well traveled we decided to keep it, thinking perhaps it might lead to some railroad station where we could take our bearings again. Trains had been passing us at regular intervals. One stopped at a station sign which read: Cosnino.

Fred and Mr. Poyen went to consult the train men. They said that Walnut Station was about six miles from Cosnino, and directly north of Turkey Tanks (which we had intended to reach by evening). Mr. and Mrs. Poyen were anxious to camp, as it was getting dark, so we drove back a short distance to a pool of water and here spent the night. We camped in separate parties but quite near. It rained some in the night, but it was not this that disturbed us.

It was the frequent passing of trains on the track so near us that kept us awake and worried "our friends in the rear."

This morning Fred found a Mexican shepherd in the woods, tending a flock of Merino sheep. We learned from him that if we followed the road down the arroyo in which we were we would come to the Turkey Tanks road. This we did, "our friends in the rear" following with anxious faces.

At ten o'clock, thanks to good luck, we came in sight of the corral and high rocks which were the landmarks of Turkey Tanks. We all felt much relieved, especially Miss McCowan, to whom traveling by wagon is a new experience. The horses were unhitched and we took our buckets and went in search of water.

In a little gulch among big smooth rocks we found a pretty pool of "agua fria." But when this water is inspected closely small living things may be seen wriggling about in it, so we do not dare drink it till [it is] boiled.

Miss McCowan took several views of the large rocks with her camera. Then she and I climbed a little hill and made a collection of Aztec pottery. After lunch we carried water over the rocks and filled our barrels.

Soon it began to rain in large drops. Mr. and Mrs. Poyen sought refuge in a deserted little cabin nearby, and Fred, Arthur, and I climbed in the wagon where we are at the present writing. Miss McCowan and Winifred were down in the gulch when it began to rain and I suppose they have found some cave or cleft in the rock for shelter.

It is raining pretty hard and is now beginning to hail. We shall start again as soon as the storm ceases.

## Wednesday, August 17

We are camped near the place called Walnut Canyon. We went off the road a little, hoping to find water in the canyon, but it was dry.

## Thursday, August 18

The road today has tended in a general northeasterly direction, and has been mostly over a rocky prairie, with red cliffs scattered over it. These cliffs seem to have had cavities washed out and present a honeycomb appearance.

The road today was strewn profusely with malapai and limestone rocks, and Miss McCowan had a chance to taste of the delights of jolting. In some places the road was like a well-worn macadamized street, the rocks were so flat and smooth.

This a.m. the boys shot at a coyote that came impudent[ly] to the road and sang to us. By and by we caught sight of a green strip in the distance which we knew to be the Little Colorado [River]. Mr. Poyen drove up beside us and asked, "How fah do you judge we ah from the rivah?"

"O, about two miles, I expect," said our driver in an easy, careless manner. But on and on we went and (as Miss McCowan remarked) the green strip seemed to get no nearer as we approached it.

Mr. Poyen became very restless and impatient and would frequently ask such question as these, "Ah you quite suah we ah on the right road?"

"O, reasonably so," Fred would answer.

"Well, don't you think it's about time we wuh getting to the rivah?"

"N-noap, hardly."

"You don't? Waal, naow, how fah do you think it is naow?"

"About two miles," said Fred, laughing. And after this our standard measurement of distance will be "two miles." And when any of us express our doubts or anxieties about the road Fred says, "I'm afraid you are catching the contagion."

Well, we reached the river about one o'clock. It was a narrow gorge filed with muddy water which the horses refused to drink. A cable extended across it for ferrying people across in times of high water.

After we left the river the road became very sandy and upgrade. It was very hard pulling, and whenever we felt so disposed we got out and walked, to save the poor, tired horses. Our next landmark was to be Volz's store, twelve miles from the river.

Four vehicles and several horse riders passed us, trotting at a surprising speed through the heavy sand, while we with our heavy load must be content to plod along slowly. Mr. and Mrs. Poyen could travel faster than we, so they kept up with the faster crowd, leaving us behind. This rather pleased us, for now we were relieved of anxiety about them.

We passed many pretty cliffs, and before reaching the store witnessed one of those glorious sunsets peculiar to Arizona.

We arrived at the [Volz] store about eight o'clock. In the yard around the small building were drawn up all the teams and wagons that had passed us. These, together with the tourists who were running back and forth from house to wagons, quite blockaded the entrance.

Finding that Mr. Volz was completely occupied with his other guests, we drove back a short distance from the house to camp. It was very dark and beginning to rain, quite a gloomy prospect for the night. We tried to fasten up the wagon sheet to the wagon for a tent but the wind was so strong that the stakes and pins persisted in coming out, so we gave it up.

Volz Trading Post at Canyon Diablo, September 9, 1906. *MS 143-11-1-998, Plate 122, Earle R. Forrest Collection, Navajoland. Museum of Northern Arizona.*

Fred was feeling bad, which greatly added to our discouragement. We threw the rolls of bedding under the half-fastened and flapping canvas, and crawled under it ourselves with the grub box, for we had not had our supper yet. We lit the candle but the wind soon extinguished it. So we fished out some bread and meat in the dark, and ate it while we all held tightly to the flying sheet over us.

As we sat thus, crouched under the low roof, someone remarked that this was the most unpleasant camp we had made and that our recollection of it in after days would afford us a great deal more enjoyment than the stern reality of the circumstances was doing then. (To which wise remark we all agreed.)

Soon the wind and rain subsided enough for us to try once more to fasten the obstinate wagon sheet, and to spread out the bedding. All night long the wind blew and the sand drifted in upon our countenances, giving us dreams of the barren Sahara. But with morning's glad light we were able to face our conditions with stronger and more cheerful hearts.

All the other tourists had slept near the store, some inside it and some outside in tents. Mr. and Mrs. Poyen lodged with a man in his tent. About a half-dozen Navajo Indians slept near the store last night. There are several shacks and cornfields in sight which I supposed are their homes.

*Friday, August 19*

---

This morning the boys led the horses to water at a near lake and we got drinking water at a well near the store. While Fred and Miss McCowan were getting a bucket of water at the well one of our fellow travelers, a lady, came to the well carrying a silver cup lined with gold, and asked them for a little "watah." Now the water in the well was not the kind usually drunk by the "bettah classes," being of a brackish hue and rich consistency, and just at that moment a jolly frog hopped from the bucket as Fred drew it up.

"O!" cried the lady with the silver cup. "I think I'll change my mind, suh," and she walked away leaving Fred and Miss McCowan shaking with suppressed laughter. Our friends started before us this morning and Mr. and Mrs. Poyen went with them.

A very old Indian woman near the store attracted our attention, and we walked up to see her. She laughed and jabbered us a hearty welcome, and made us understand by sign language that she was both deaf and blind. A little fat Indian lad directed her tottering steps. Her hair was very white and the sharp claws at the ends of her long, bony fingers gave her a rather inhuman appearance. Miss McCowan succeeded in getting a snapshot of her.

Fred gained permission to leave a sack of grain at the store till we shall come back from the Indian villages.

The road was sandy again and we went very slowly. The country all around was barren, save for sagebrush and cactus, and the sun's rays felt very warm, reminding us slightly of the deserts of the Salt River Valley.

Far in the distance we saw a deep-green tree which seemed to promise that water was near it. As the horses were very thirsty, we drove towards the tree. The journey proved to be a long, sandy, three-mile chase. We girls got out and walked ahead as we neared the tree and found a large, pretty lake which almost repaid us for our trouble in reaching it.

After the horses had drunk their fill we started back to our road. For quite a while we couldn't find it and wandered about quite lost over rocks and sand, with no signs of civilization around us. Arthur and I gathered quite a number of specimens of pottery, which lay thick upon the ground. We were very thankful when we got back on our road and now began to look for Burro Springs.

About six o'clock we passed a white man camped with two horses and a burro. We asked him how far it was to Burro Springs. There were several Hopi Indians standing about his camp, and he told us that one of them had brought him water in a short time. So we concluded we must be near the springs. We drove on a few hundred yards, and whom should we see but our friends the Poyens! And *right* glad we were to see them again.

Their horses had given out so they were forced to stop and camp. Indians were grouped about them, primitive and intelligent-looking Hopis. They brought us dry sagebrush (the only wood procurable in that desert spot) and helped us start a fire.

One carried armloads of green corn for the horses. They were all very pleasant and friendly. The women wear their hair parted and brought down around their necks in long wrapped bunches (a sign that they are married) and carry their babies upon their backs, with their little heads sticking out at the top of the mother's blanket.

One young woman immediately aroused our interest, both on account of her ability to speak English and her remarkable beauty. Her black eyes shone like stars, and her white teeth showed very pretty when she smiled. She carried a baby under her blanket. She said she and her husband had both attended the Indian school at Keam's Canyon several years ago. She could talk better English than any of the others and [she] remembered that her English name given her at school was Ethel.

We quite fell in love with her, especially Fred. Indeed, we were afraid we could not induce Fred away from the Springs on account of this bewitching Indian maid! There

First camp leaving Canyon Diablo, after crossing Little Colorado River, September 2, 1906. *MS 143-11-14-999, Plate 3. Earle R. Forrest Collection, Hopiland. Museum of Northern Arizona.*

Volz party camp en route to Snake Dance at Oraibi, September 3, 1906. *MS 143-11-1-1000, Plate 123. Earle R. Forrest Collection, Navajoland. Museum of Northern Arizona.*

Hopi woman and child visiting camp, September 3, 1906. *MS 143-11-14-1001, Plate 5. Earle R. Forrest Collection, Hopiland. Museum of Northern Arizona.*

were about twenty Indians at the Springs, all related, they said. Their home was at the nearest Hopi village, Shungopavi, but they had come to the springs to raise corn. We found the spring under the side of a rocky cliff. The water was good, but very scarce.

The Indians lingered about our camp until dark and came flocking in next morning with smiling faces, jabbering and laughing, and gathering up tin cans, scraps of paper, etc., about the camp. We asked them a great many questions about the situation and distances of the different Indian villages, but couldn't get much satisfactory information from them. They told us that Shungopavi was three miles away.

Mr. and Mrs. Poyen started before us for Oraibi, as they did not care to visit the other villages. It took us quite a while to form our plans for visiting the different villages and to engage one of the Indians as a guide for three days of our trip. Ethel's husband seemed to speak English best of all the men, and [he] was willing to guide us for one dollar per day. So we sent him to pack his pony and we packed up.

After we had started Ethel and her father came running down the slope from their houses to tell us that the father, Anoya, who was chief of the tribe, would go with us afoot until our guide should have caught his pony and overtaken us. So we bid Ethel adieu and Anoya followed us.

But I was about to forget to say that we had other company from Burro Springs—the lonely little man with the two horses and a burro. Mr. O'Toole was his name, and he promised to be a very pleasant and kind companion.

Soon our guide appeared on his pony, dressed in a red calico shirt, blue overalls, slouched hat, moccasins, and a belt of large, tin shells. These men all wear their hair twisted in a knot and tied behind, with long straight bangs on front and sides.

The distance to Shungopavi proved to be about twelve miles instead of three, so it was about four o'clock before we arrived there. We had been watching the high, rocky mesa, however, upon which it is built, ever since we started from the springs. Even when we reached the foot of it we could not see the village because it is built back from the ledge. Besides this, the houses are the same color as the mesa.

All the Hopi villages are built upon high mesas. This one must have been about 1,500 feet high and very rocky.

Mr. O'Toole stayed in camp with our horses and wagon and our guide led the rest of us up the trail to the village. O! but it was romantic! Everything looked so old and historic. First we climbed over rolling hills worn smooth by the daily tread of sheep until we reached the spring which comes bubbling out of the rocks and empties into a pond. We were tired and thirsty and the cool, sweet water was very gratifying to us.

Not far from the spring was a large square excavation like a well with a little stagnant water in it. Stone steps led to the bottom, and at the water's edge was planted a curious stick wrapped with red cord and mounted by a feather. Our guide told us that this feather was sacred and was used to attract snakes to the well, to be caught for the dance.

Our path soon became steeper and rockier. In many places it was a regular stone stairway, worn smooth by the tread of the villagers. At last, after much puffing and blowing, we gained the summit and walked to the village which was built about one hundred yards from the edge of the mesa. What a sight it was!

The houses built of stone and adobe were of the same color as the cliffs. They were nearly all two or three stories high, with stone steps or ladders ascending to the tops. The dogs began to bark, the chickens to crow, and the whole population put their heads out of the windows or stepped out upon the housetops to get a better view of us. They nodded and smiled, and insisted upon shaking hands when this was possible.

Our guide first led us into a clean room whitewashed on the outside, which he said was his home. There seemed to be no one in the house, so we asked him where his people were. He replied, "I tink maybe my mother hass kon to ket wut." We tried to convince him that it was not right for the women to be the wood carriers, but he only laughed and shook his head. (Probably he thought it was none of our business.)

We moved about the large room and examined everything freely. Small lofts were built about the room in which were stowed piles of corn, the principal living of the Hopis. Many curious objects hung upon the walls, such as hideous wooden idols of dolls, bright baskets, fox and badger skins, etc. Large blankets (some woven from rabbit skins) lay about upon the stone floor.

In one corner of the room was a long, low bin, in the sloping sides of which were fastened three large, flat stones which are used in grinding corn. There were two fireplaces in the room, and over a fire in one hung a black kettle, probably containing the evening meal. There were also a cook stove and several other modern articles such as an old coffee mill, tin cups, etc., which looked rather out of place amid such primitive surroundings. We afterwards learned the cook stoves had been furnished the Indians by the government.

Soon there came into the house a woman who we at once decided was our guide's sister-in-law on account of her great likeness to Ethel. She was even more attractive in fact than Ethel and had the brightest eyes I think I have ever seen. From the warmth with which she and her baby were greeted by her brother-in-law we suspected that she was also his wife, and [we] asked him about it. He seemed rather embarrassed and said that Hopi men had only one wife apiece.

As we walked out of the house a bent and aged woman climbed the ladder and let fall from her back a great bundle of wood, upon the upper veranda. Her hair was white and her swarthy skin was wrinkled. We knew by the tone of her voice that she was complaining of her long, weary struggle up the mesa with her great load.

When our guide saw her he greeted her with kind words but did not even touch her hand. He now went to visit several of his friends and left us to go where we would. We saw through the door of an upper room some women weaving baskets, and climbed up to see them work. But as soon as we had entered their house and asked for the baskets they began to laugh roguishly at us and to talk to each other. They had hidden their precious baskets and could not be persuaded to produce them, fearing, I suppose, that we should learn the art.

These women had their papooses wrapped and strapped to a board in typically Indian fashion. Through the narrow streets naked children frisked about and chased one another for our special benefit. The unmarried girls wore their hair in two large glossy rolls above each ear. This was an infallible sign of their maidenhood, while the married women were known from the two thick twists hanging over the shoulders.

I remember that we were very tired and hungry when we reached the valley. We feared it should rain before we could eat supper, but only a few drops fell. We cooked rabbits that Fred had shot and boiled Irish potatoes, and I'll tell you, never did supper taste better!

Our guide evidently thought so, too, and soon his spirits had risen to such a high pitch that when we besought him again to tell us his name (theretofore he had refused)

Hopi maidens, September 5, 1906. *MS 143-11-14-1024, Plate 27. Earle R. Forrest Collection, Hopiland. Museum of Northern Arizona.*

this time he complied and said his name was "Yo-yo-hung-awah." And then such a time as we had trying to pronounce it! He kept repeating it, and we kept practicing it until we could each say it with the proper accent.

## Saturday, August 20

---

We slept under the tent last night. This morning we rode the horses to the spring to water them. Mr. O'Toole let me ride his pretty black pony, Julia—a fine riding horse. There are several small gardens around the spring where corn and potatoes are raised, and more gardens near the village, although we did not see them yesterday.

It was late ere we were started for the next two villages, Shipaulovi and Mishongnovi. These two are situated on the same [Second] mesa and not far from Shungopavi. Fred and I did not visit these villages but stayed below in the wagon while Mr. O'Toole accompanied the rest to the mesa, Winifred and Miss McCowan riding the black pony.

While we sat waiting some Indian men passed us, bounding over the rocks at a great rate. They were not much "put on" and were all painted and ornamented with plumes. In their hands they carried each a bunch of sacred feathers and a sack.

One man and a small boy stopped at our wagon and we asked them what they were going to do. The boy (who had evidently been to school) replied that they were starting out to hunt rattlesnakes for their village dance, which was to occur again at Shipaulovi in five days. The man spoke to the boy, who then rather unwillingly asked us for tobacco.

As we could not accommodate them in this way we gave them matches, which are always acceptable to them. Then they sped away and were soon lost from sight. Soon we heard a savage whoop, and looking in the direction the men had gone [we] saw several of them meet and stoop among the rocks. Evidently they had found a sacred reptile.

A flock of black goats and sheep passed by, being driven

to graze in the valley. An old woman and a little girl followed, carrying green peaches in their blankets. They insisted that we take some. Fred was a little afraid we should get stone bruised from handling them, but we ventured to take one apiece for a souvenir. Peach trees seem to thrive quite well on the level ground and it seems a pity that the fruit is not allowed to ripen.

When the folks returned from visiting Shipaulovi and Mishongnovi they informed us that the corn dance at Walpi was to occur at sunset, so we made haste to reach Walpi, which was about eighteen miles away. The country we passed through was much of a sameness—heavy sand with no vegetation but weeds and a little grass, and here and there a little farm of corn, peach trees, and potatoes.

At about four o'clock we reached Walpi; that is, we got as near to the [First] mesa as possible with a wagon and camped among a little cluster of peach trees. Our guide con-

Walpi Indian Village. San Francisco Peaks in background, c. 1900.
*Arizona Historical Society/Pioneer Museum, Flagstaff. NAPHS #742-4.*

sented to remain with our goods while we should go to the village.

Walpi is not so difficult of approach as the other pueblos we had visited, nor so high. But the population is greater. I suppose it must have been about six hundred. Its elevation above the surrounding country is estimated at 350 feet. The houses are set back only a few yards from the edge of the rocky cliff, leaving a long space in which the ceremonials are performed.

The dancers had not yet arrived, having gone into the valley for sacred water. We could see them far down in the distance creeping along in solemn procession and looking like as many sheep or cattle. We had ample time to visit the houses of the village before they reached the summit.

Whether in honor of the occasion or not, the inhabitants of this village were as a rule dressed better than those at Shipaulovi. There were about twenty-five white people assembled to see the show, many of them from Keam's Canyon. Many had cameras and while [they were] waiting took views of the inhabitants.

We climbed into an upper room where we had heard that the ceremonial altar was situated. Here were four small boys decorated with feathers, beads, and paint frisking about, impatient for their part in the performance. The altar consisted of many mystic symbols arrayed upon the floor, too complicated for my description. It was guarded by a stern-looking old man and a decorated young man, who forbade us to touch anything about the sacred spot or to even make a drawing of the different objects in the altar.

At about six o'clock we all gathered about the edge of the cliff to watch the dancers wind slowly up the slope. There were thirty-six of them. The priest led the procession, naked to the waist, from which hung a short black and white blanket.

On his head he wore a white turban mounted by two green horns and covered with white feathers. His shoulders and breast were painted white, and white bands of paint extended around his legs. Below his knees were hoops of basketwork and rattles of turtle shells. He carried a bowl of sacred meal. When they reached the top of the mesa he ran ahead and sprinkled it upon the ground in the shape of a rain cloud (supposed to be, at least).

Then the procession halted, standing six abreast. In the first row was the asperger, a white-haired man whose duty it was to scatter upon the heads of his fellow Indians the sacred water which he carried in a bowl. Two maidens in bridal costume with their chins painted black were also in the front row, and between them a little boy, highly painted. The other men were dressed in red and white blankets, their long hair hanging, and three sunflowers upon their heads. There was a spot of white paint on each cheek, and white paint extending down their legs.

The priest scattered the meal in a shape something like this figure, representing the rain clouds.

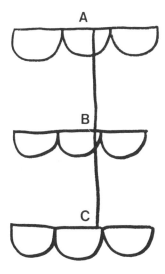

When the front row had stopped a few steps before "A" the three children, who each carried upon a stick a braided circle of reeds, threw them one at a time upon the three rings of the meal, the priest assisting in placing them there. Then they advanced and picked them up with their sticks, threw them to "B,"advanced and picked them up, and so on to "C."

Meanwhile, the dancers behind them chanted a weird strain, and two warriors in the rear whirled their whips in the air, making a whizzing sound. Another meal picture was made similar to the first, and the whole performance was repeated.

The two girls and one boy, in giving their ring offerings to the rain clouds, represent their idea of the combined male and female element in their prayers for rain.

They next stopped before a little shack covered with cottonwood boughs and sang their monotonous prayer songs for about an hour, the priest all the while keeping time with his foot, the others shaking the rattles that they carried, and the asperger scattering sacred water about profusely. When they had ended their prayers they each deposited an offering of a cornstalk inside the shack.

The priest covered up the opening with brush and mud to prevent the inquisitive from peeping into it. This done, they filed away through a narrow alley to perform their private ceremony at the altar, and as far as we were concerned the dance was ended.

There are two other villages on the Walpi mesa, Sichomavi and Tewa. Winifred, Miss McCowan, and Arthur went with some other visitors to see the villages, and Fred and I wended our way down the valley. We had supper ready when they returned, and of course we were all very hungry. Yo-yo-hung-awah had gathered some good peach wood and had the fire ready to light when we returned.

We told him he was a good boy, which seemed to please

him very much. Fred gave him permission to go back to Burro Springs now, since there would be many other whites going to Oraibi tomorrow, and the road would be plain. But he said he wanted to go with us another day.

## Sunday, August 21

This morning we rode about two miles to find water for the horses. I rode Nellie bareback and was left far behind the others all the way.

We found good water at a spring where other white travelers had camped in empty government houses. There are about thirty-five of these houses scattered about the foot of the Walpi mesa. They were built by the government for the use of the Indians, but most of the Indians prefer to live in their pueblos. So most of the houses are empty, except a few [that are] inhabited by teachers and missionaries.

It must have been very late in the morning when we started for Oraibi. Our fellow travelers had all started before us. We arrived here (at Oraibi) about three o'clock. The road from Walpi was mostly down steep hills and through sand. We read in *The Old Curiosity Shop* and *Tales from McClure's* and sang some to pass away the time.

Oraibi is the largest of the villages, having about seven hundred inhabitants. The mesa is quite long. Only the one village is upon it. There are about twelve government houses at the foot of the mesa made of adobe, with red roofs. Indians live in some of them but there were enough empty ones to house all the white visitors.

We obtained permission to camp in an unfinished house of four rooms, all very clean and new. An Indian kindly offered us the use of his stove, table, and chairs in his house nearby, but as we had already carried our things into this house we declined his offer and built our campfire near this house. There is an odor about all the Indian houses that is not the most appetizing.

We feel quite "tony" in our new house. Winifred and Miss McCowan have gone up to the village to see a sunset dance. Artie has gone to the store about four miles away on Mr. O'Toole's pony to get flour. Fred has unhitched the horses and is negotiating with some Indians for corn fodder.

We carried our bedding, grub box, etc., into the house. In one room there are some long boards laid across two tall trestles, making a first-rate table for us. I have washed the dishes and we will soon get supper.

Hopi men at foot of Third Mesa, side of Oraibi, September 4, 1906. *MS 143-11-1002, Plate 6. Earle R. Forrest Collection, Hopiland. Museum of Northern Arizona.*

## Monday, August 22

We had many Indian visitors, who pried through the house as if they were quite at home. After supper a Mr. Allen and a Mr. Consor came over and talked with us for a while. We lit a candle and sat about our bedroom, on the bedding and in the windows.

These two men are interested in the Indian School at Keam's Canyon. Consequently [they] could tell some very interesting stories and customs of the different tribes. They told us that the Navajo men and their mothers-in-law never look at each other's faces, believing they would die if they should. The Navajos live in huts on the level ground and are a roving tribe. If they think one of their family is about to die they shut up the house and leave it, never opening it again. The Hopis bury their dead in crevices among the rocks.

When Arthur returned from the store he had no flour because, he said, the reservation law prohibits the store from selling on Sunday. We went again this morning and this time succeeded in getting some.

We have been lying around, reading, and writing this morning. There was a fourteen-mile race by the Indians at sunrise which we did not see. There will be no other ceremonies until this evening at sunset when the big snake dance will occur. Of course we will all take that in.

## Tuesday, August 23

---

It was reported that the dance would occur at six o'clock, which is the usual hour for the evening dances. Miss McCowan wanted to buy some baskets and take some views of the village, so she started to the village about four o'clock. But the rest of us didn't care to go so soon, so Fred and Winifred took the horses to water.

When they returned we started up, about five o'clock, thinking we should have ample time. But upon reaching the village we learned to our extreme disappointment that the wonderful snake dance was over and that the snakes had been turned loose. The snake men had become impatient and refused to wait until the appointed time.

The following account was written by Miss McCowan, who was as much disappointed as we ourselves that we missed the dance, and who kindly offered me her description of the ceremony:

> I was sitting comfortably talking to several people when the antelope men came out of their kiva, nine of them, painted black as to the lower part of the face with a white line along the upper edge of black; arms painted black to the elbow, with white lightning, white below to the wrists, legs white from ankle to knee, black above with white lightning. They wore kilts and a fox skin hanging down behind, red moccasins, strings of beads with a beautiful iridescent shell hanging down in front. A skein of black yarn went over the right shoulder and under the left arm. Each carried a flat rattler.

*The first one had a red bag of sacred meal.*

*They went round in a circle four times, sprinkling sacred meal on the board in front of the kisi and stamping on it. Then they ranged themselves in front of the kisi and waited for the snake men, who soon came out of their kiva. Their faces were painted black to above the eyebrows and they had brown patches of paint on arms, shoulders, breasts, and legs. They wore kilts and moccasins, and feathers in their hair. They carried snake whips and two long eagle feathers in the right hand and a bag of sacred meal in the left.*

*After dancing some time the snake men, waving their whips from right to left and then back again, and the antelopes shook their rattles. The snake men arranged themselves in twos and with two single ones. These latter were to gather up the snakes as they were put on the ground. The foremost one of each group stooped at the opening of the kisi, reached in, got a snake, went on, putting it near the neck and in his mouth and holding it by both hands along the body. The second of the two put his left hand on the left shoulder of the other and with the whip in his right hand stroked the back of the snake carrier.*

*After going around the circle, the snake man put down his snake and got another. The gatherers sprinkled sacred meal over the snake, stroked him if restless with the whip, and dex-*

*terously grabbed him. When the gatherer had
a number of snakes in his hand he gave them
to the antelope men to hold. The neophyte,
about six years old, had three of the long ones,
but they weren't rattlers.*

*After they had carried all the snakes in their
mouths they went off a little distance, formed
a circle, threw all the snakes in a heap on the
ground, sprinkled sacred meal over them, the
women spat on them, and then the snake
priests grabbed as many as they could and
went in different directions down the mesa to
liberate the snakes.*

*Two of the priests didn't get any snakes, so
they went back to the kisi, circled around four
times, sprinkling the meal on the board and
stamping on it, then they went to their kiva.
When the snake men came back from carrying
the snakes away they went to their kiva and
washed themselves, then came up and drank
the emetic the women had prepared and
brought to them.*

*I didn't watch the subsequent proceeding, but
the children came to the village just in time to
witness that performance. The antelopes who
had remained in a line all this time did their
four circles and departed to their kiva.*

We were determined to see all that we could and were
overjoyed to learn that the snake men would perform the
last act of the drama in our presence. They put their heads

into the large bowls of the emetic and drank deeply, then walked to the edge of the kiva or sanctuary and performed the remainder of the ceremony.

There were about thirty white visitors, many of whom we became acquainted with. Most of the men had cameras, and took views of the performers in this last solemn act. One man had a kinetoscope, which took several continuous views per second.

When the snake men had completely emptied their stomachs the performance was ended and we descended the mountain.

Returning from Snake Dance at Oraibi, September 6, 1906. *MS 143-11-1-1048, Plate 130. Earle R. Forrest Collection, Navajoland. Museum of Northern Arizona.*

Tuesday morning at an early hour we started on our homeward journey for the pines of Flagstaff. Mr. O'Toole went with us, but Mr. and Mrs. Poyen kept with some of the other crowd. We camped about six miles before we got to Volz's store.

Wednesday morning we drove to the store, where some of our fellow travelers had stopped, among them [the] Poyens. Fred bought a blanket here. Miss McCowan took a few views and we watered the horses. Then we went on, hoping to reach the river in the evening. To our disappointment none of the sand had disappeared since we traveled the road before. We reached the river at dusk and found it risen, so [we] camped before trying to cross.

Thursday morning Fred woke us all early. We packed up and greased the wagon in a great hurry. We didn't even wait to eat breakfast in our eagerness to be off. Mr. and Mrs. Poyen had overtaken us and camped near us. They were very nervous and excited about crossing the river, and I think all of us were a little afraid.

Fred left us on the bank while he plunged into the dark waters with the wagon. We waited, almost breathless, till he had safely reached the shore. He came back to us on the little cable car and ferried us across. Mr. and Mrs. Poyen had to ferry all their goods across, as the river was too high for their low buckboard to keep dry.

When the whole party, even to the little pack burro, were safely across, we heaved a sigh of relief. That night at ten o'clock we reached Turkey Tanks. The horses became so weak that for a mile or two we walked behind the wagon and pushed to help them. We were indeed very glad to get to Turkey Tanks where we could get water.

Next morning we didn't get started very early, having only sixteen miles before us. However, Vic was so worn out that we had to go very slowly, and it was about six o'clock when we waited in front of the Flagstaff post office for our mail. We left Miss McCowan at her boarding place and camped in our same old spot. We will probably start from Flagstaff Saturday afternoon, August 27.

*Sunday, August 28*

---

I am sitting in the wagon waiting till the boys hitch the horses. Fred just now reminded us that this is Sunday, and we remarked that Sunday seems like any other day to us, except that we read our Sunday School quarterly then.

We drove from Flagstaff yesterday afternoon and camped five miles southwest. There is an abundance of grass for the horses and a forest of pines for the campfire, [and] large fallen logs for seats, some with hollows of water in them which we use for wash basins, watering troughs, etc. So we have every convenience for camping that one could desire.

The dew fell heavily last night and those of us who left our clothes on the log had to dry [them] by the campfire this morning. Vic was still weak and unable to travel fast yesterday, so we camped early in hopes that after a few hours of rest and plenty of good grass she would be strengthened by this morning.

Miss McCowan lent us *The Mill on the Floss* to read on our way home. She also gave us her photo, which we prize greatly. Vic seemed just as weak as ever, so we couldn't go far today.

We came over very beautiful country, up and down grassy hills covered with pines and flowers with an occasional lumber camp or log dwelling. We read in our book as much as the condition of the roads permitted. In one shady glen we found running water, about thirteen miles from Flagstaff. We drove to the top of the hill beyond it, where we are now camped.

It was about two o'clock when we arrived here, and we spent the afternoon reading under the pine trees. Winifred and I went to a rocky nook in the stream and had a delightful bath. We made a large fire and cooked beans, and boiled potatoes with the skins on. When we ate supper we thought potatoes never had tasted so good.

A man, old lady, and little boy passed in a wagon, headed our way. Fred told the man about our sick horse and received full instructions from the old lady in regard to the best remedies. The man's name was Mr. [Robert] Finnie of Soda Springs, an uncle of Miss Finnie, whom we had met at Flagstaff. Fred asked him about the possibility of getting another horse at Soda Springs or at [John L.] Munds' ranch, eight miles from here.

Mr. Finnie thought it probable that Mr. Munds could let us have a horse, and offered to take Fred with him at once to inquire. But Fred thinks we can get to Munds' tomorrow with Victoria if we give her a long rest and let her eat all the grass she wants.

We noticed a camping outfit stop across the brook this afternoon, and while we were eating supper a man and lady from that camp passed our camp on their way home from a stroll through the woods, each carrying a gun. They said they were headed towards Beaver Creek from Flagstaff. We noticed that they have put up a tent. Fred says he has extreme pity for people who make so much trouble for themselves as to set up a tent every day.

The moon and stars are coming out, and I am glad to think that we may sleep under the open sky tonight. I love to watch the stars and white sailing clouds when I lie down. The tall pines stand about us so straight and seem to keep watch over us while we sleep.

*Monday, August 29*

---

The dew fell heavily again last night and everything was damp this morning. When Winifred and I awoke there was a bright fire burning and Fred had put the little black bucket on the fire to heat water for mush.

After breakfast I said to Winifred in imitation of our home talk, "I'll wash the dishes and clean up the house if you will do the washing." It was agreed upon one condition, that I should also scrub the kitchen floor. Our thoughts had naturally turned towards home as soon as our wagon had turned from Flagstaff in that direction, so we kept up the play, calling upon an imaginary Nat for wood and an imaginary Mildred for various small services. Fred hung a clothesline and our washing was out at an early hour, testifying to our great thrift.

We passed the morning reading, and after dinner packed our things and started off. Vic traveled pretty well and we walked up all the hills. We arrived at a ranch which we suppose is Munds' and have camped near a ditch of water.

After we ate supper Fred heated some water and he and Winifred gave the sick horse a warm bath. Fred has now taken her to water. After she drinks he will feed her some boiled barley, which I hear cooking now. Nothing is too good for a sick horse, you know.

There is a field of small yellow sunflowers to my left, very pretty against the dark green of the pines. Arthur is making some sassafras tea, which must be done, judging from the fragrance in the air.

## Tuesday, August 30

We started quite early this morning and Vic pulled very well. We walked up the hills which occurred at frequent intervals and were mostly long and steep. The road was rocky, so that we could read very little. At noon we camped under a pine tree and ate bread and butter and beans, a very good dinner.

Early in the afternoon we passed a man camped by the road. He was on his way from Oak Creek to Flagstaff and had a load of watermelons. Fred purchased a small one for forty cents, and visions of watermelon for supper filled the afternoon with pleasant thoughts for us.

Gradually the pines began to dwindle down, and oaks and cedars to cover the hills. A fat rattler on a rock by the road attracted our attention. Fred killed it and amputated six pairs of rattles from it.

When we reached the top of a hill Winifred and I, who were walking ahead of the wagon, paused to look at a grand sight. To the west a long, blue range lay, on the slope of which we could see the smoke from Jerome mines. Nearer to us stretched the Mogollon Range, beyond which lay the Verde Valley. To the north was a rocky cliff much like those

Jerome, 1900. *Sharlot Hall Museum Library/Archives, Prescott, Arizona.* (*XM-479p.*)

in the Grand Canyon. This cliff marked the position of Oak Creek.

While we were admiring the grandeur of the sight, Fred called to us to "Wait for the wagon," and when he had over-taken us he said, "I wish to dilate a little upon this beautiful scenery."

So we climbed in and he explained to us the relative positions and distances of the points around us, and laid further plans for our journey home. We met several wagons and horsemen and found some difficulty in passing over the rocky hills. At every ravine Fred would think, "Surely *this* is Rattlesnake Tanks," but each time it would prove to be only a dry gorge.

On a tree by the roadside hung a dead coyote grinning hideously at us. On it were several placards bearing such writings as, "Butcher shop! Fine Fresh Meat! Don't be a hog, and leave some for the next comer!" etc., with several very clever verses attached, telling of the life and death of the poor coyote.

About four o'clock we camped on a hillside amid the cedars and oaks. We were rather pleased to be among the cedars again. Some of our happiest camps have been among them, on account of the jolly big fires we could build of the dead cedar wood. We dragged a dead tree near to the wagon for fuel and then sat down on the rolls of bedding and carved the watermelon. It was quite a treat. But do not suppose for a moment that we ate it all at once. O, no! For melon at two cents per pound is far more "fillin'" than at one-half cent.

Vic seems to feel almost as well as usual. Fred is build-ing a fire now and Sister is preparing to boil some potatoes. The boys killed a squirrel this afternoon with the help of Trilby, but Winifred thinks squirrel and watermelon in the same day would be too extravagant living for us, so we shall keep the squirrel for breakfast.

There are clouds gathering and I fear we shall have to hoist our canvas.

## Wednesday, August 31

---

It began to rain before our supper was quite ready. We placed the table inside the wagon sheet upon the rolls of bedding and ate supper very comfortably, all the cozier for the pattering rain outside. After supper we packed the dishes in the lunch box—we couldn't think of washing them at a time like this—and spread out the bedding to sit upon.

We read in our book by candlelight until we were sleepy. The rain all this time was coming down in heavy torrents and we had to pile up the dirt in a ridge to keep the floor of our dwelling dry. But before we were asleep the moon was shining peacefully and all was quiet. We slept quite warm and dry.

Towards morning it began to rain again and I awoke to hear Fred throwing up a trench outside the tent. We all arose and dressed, but, finding everything else wet and uninviting, we took off our shoes and crawled back under the covers. But what were we to do! We could sleep no longer and it was not light enough to read. We couldn't cook breakfast, but there was the remainder of the watermelon! What more pleasant occupation than eating watermelon, especially under our present circumstances, which had a rather depressing influence upon our spirits.

When this course was ended we each had a piece of bread and butter and declared ourselves to have sumptuously breakfasted. We climbed into the wagon and read some more of Maggie's and Tom's troubles. A very funny chapter about Bob Jokem put us in a good humor, and we decided that although the rain was pouring down we could be happy so long as we were all well and our horses kept strong.

About eight o'clock the rain ceased and we packed up and started before another shower could catch us. The roads were very muddy and slick. Winifred, Arthur and I tried to walk, but after accumulating enough soil upon our shoes to grow a field of corn, [we] gave it up as a bad job and Fred let us get into the wagon. Some of the way was reading road. The book is so interesting that we are afraid we shall finish it too soon.

About five o'clock we arrived at Soda Springs. Mr. Finnie lives here in a very comfortable-looking house and grows fruit, corn, etc. A creek flows through his farm and on its banks grow sycamore trees and wild grapevines.

We are camped below Mr. Finnie's place on the bank of the [Beaver] creek, which has risen during the recent rains and rushes in a swift torrent. Mr. and Mrs. Willis of Phoenix are camping in Mr. Finnie's farm yard. They passed our camp a few minutes ago. They told us that they arrived here last Friday and have been rained upon daily ever since.

## Thursday, September 1

---

This morning we packed up, ready to start, and walked to Mr Finnie's. It is a very home-like place. The house is of white sandstone, trimmed in red stone. In the rear is a screened porch covered with hop vine, and pots of house plants stand within.

We crossed the creek upon a log and went through the orchard of apple, prune, and plum trees till we came to the springs. Amid a thicket of trees is a small pool of mineral

Soda Springs, Finnie Ranch. *Courtesy of The Southwest Museum, Los Angeles, California. Photo #P.4235, George Wharton James Collection.*

water bubbling up through the sand. We tasted of it and thought we should prefer to drink muddy creek water. Arthur couldn't tear himself away until he had jumped into the springs.

The water was clear and cool and not deep, except in certain places where the sand was soft. But these places were not dangerous because it is impossible to sink in the soda water. Mr. Finnie intends to build a hotel and sanitarium near the springs at some time.

When we returned to the house Fred bought some corn and a pan of large rosy apples, whose delicious flavor carried our minds back to our Missouri days. We went to the wagon and started.

We stopped at a farm house where Fred bought some alfalfa hay, watermelons, cabbage, and some arrowheads from a manly little fellow who seemed to feel great responsibility and importance in being left with the care of the farm during his father's absence.

We stopped at Montezuma's Well for a few moments. It is simply a large hole in the ground about 150 yards across at [the] top and narrower at the water's edge, which must be sixty feet from [the] top. It is said that the bottom has never been reached. There were several small dwellings of an ancient people on the sides of the well, and the entrance to a cave, but we hurried on without exploring these.

At noon we stopped on the desert and sampled a watermelon while the horses rested. Greasewood, cactus, and mesquite shrubs made the country look like a Salt River Valley desert. The sun felt a little warm, too, making us think the more of Phoenix.

This p.m. the roads were both good and bad—smooth reading roads in some places and rocks and holes in others. We crossed a pretty vale through which flowed a creek called "Dry Beaver," not so dry as some things now, however.

At last we got to the cliffs of Montezuma's Castle. We left the wagon and horses tied to a mesquite tree and walked

Montezuma's Castle, c. 1900. *Sharlot Hall Museum Library/Archives, Prescott, Arizona. (IN-PR 1424pc.)*

to the castle about one-half mile away. We had to cross a little creek three times and the rocky bottom felt very sharp to our bare feet. We climbed four ladders (not prehistoric), and reached the rooms of the cliff dwellings. There were perhaps twenty rooms, bare and lonely, with an undelicious smell savoring of dead rats or mountain lions.

We registered our names in a book for that purpose, and saw some very familiar signatures of Phoenix people. We couldn't tarry here long, for we must get across the Verde River before dark. After repeating the painful crossing over the sharp rocks of the creek, we reached the wagon.

We jogged over the hills and reached the river at dusk.

Crossing the Verde River at Camp Verde, 1903. *Arizona Historical Society/Pioneer Museum, Flagstaff. NAPHS #32-1168. (George Hochderffer Collection).*

Before we crossed we stopped at a farm house and bought a hard-shelled squash and some sugar cane. A man with a light rig and a pony drove up behind us and we asked him to cross first, to see how it went. The river was not very deep, nor wide, nor scary, but somehow we felt nearer home when we had crossed and pulled up into Camp Verde on the other side.

Camp Verde is an old military post with about fifteen quarter houses, now used for family dwellings. We camped near a long, empty house. Fred walked over to the post office, and Artie and I sat down to enjoy the sugar cane.

Adjutant's Office, Camp Verde, c. 1900. *Sharlot Hall Museum Library/ Archives, Prescott, Arizona. (Mil 168P.)*

## Friday, September 2

We slept by the wagon, and when we woke this morning Fred had built a fire in the fireplace of the empty house. We ate some watermelon as an appetizer and then set our table in the old house and had breakfast. We decided that now was as good a time as any to give Trilby away. (Mrs. Ambler, in giving us the dog, had made us promise not to bring her home again.)

Arthur took her away. He first tried to give her to a white man, but after he had discoursed at length to him upon her merits as watch and hunting dog the man said, "Well, why don't you keep her yourself, if she's such a good dog? I've no use for her."

Artie then took her to a Mexican who seemed glad to keep her. He tied her in his back yard, but she broke loose and soon found the way back to our camp. This was too bad, for now Arthur had to return her to her new master and endure the agony of a second parting. As we passed the home of the Mexican we heard her barking piteously and felt sorry to leave her.

We passed some thrifty-looking farms before we left the [Verde] valley and had good reading roads for a while. But soon we climbed into the hills and for the rest of the day our road was upgrade, winding around the mountains among some beautiful scenery. We could see nothing beyond the hills above and in front of us.

The vegetation was cedar, spruce, scrub oak, small cactus, mesquite, etc. We crossed twelve times a rocky stream that wound about through a divide in the mountains, called Copper Canyon. On the banks of this stream grew tall sycamores, wild grapevines and mountain-ash trees. We stopped at one of these crossings and ate dinner on the rocks while the horses rested.

Then came one of our very long, steep hills and we "chilluns" stayed out to walk up. We met a man who said we could soon be at the top and would then begin to go downhill. We all felt glad when we reached the top and could get a view of the distant country.

About five o'clock we arrived at the [George W.] Hance ranch, owned by a brother of the Mr. Hance at Grand Canyon. After Fred had watered the horses we drove on a little till we came to some good grass.

We had no sooner become thoroughly camped than a man in a wagon drove up and asked if we wanted to buy some honey. He was on his way back to Middle Verde from Prescott where he had been peddling his produce (honey and raisins). We "chilluns" all clamored for "mountain honey," so Fred said he'd take some, just to please us, you know. The man lifted out his can to pour some into the pan Fred held, but to his surprise the can was almost empty.

"Well, now! I guess them fellers tuck it all," he said. "But you just take the can and melt it on the fire and you're welcome to all you kin get out."

Fred bought some seedless raisins of him, and drained a pint or two of honey from the can. It was a wild and very delicious flavor. We hope it will not "dew" tonight and make our bedding wet again, for it has just thoroughly dried since the rain among the cedars.

## Saturday, September 3

The horses had all the grass they could eat last night, and appreciated it, too. It "did" [dew], but we don't care a bit. Our beds will be nice and cool to sleep on tonight. [We] started rather early this morning. Today we went over rolling hills with little vegetation except grass, prickly pears, mesquite, and oak scrubs.

[We] found water for the horses in a creek at Cedar Corral near a deserted house. At noon the boys turned the horses loose to eat grass, and we ate our last watermelon. While we ate it we discussed and criticized *The Mill on the Floss*, which we finished reading this morning.

This afternoon we planned to surprise the folks at home at our return. We could camp at the Arizona Canal in the evening and at about one o'clock in the morning we would start for home by the light of the moon, arriving there before the folks were awake.

We would tie the horses, slip around to the parlor window with our shoes off, take down the screen, climb into the parlor and wake the sleepers with "Home, Sweet Home." It gave us much pleasure to plan this little surprise.

Vic soon began to droop and we looked forward to

reaching each hilltop, expecting to see Cordes Station beyond. We came into the Black Canyon road and soon saw a sign like this: "PHOENIX 75 miles" nailed to a mesquite tree. This was gratifying to us and we thought surely Cordes was not far away. But on account of Victoria (she was staggering along with her nose almost touching the ground) we thought we had better stop till morning.

So here we are on the top of a hill inhabited by only wild cows and horses. Fred gave Vic all the water in the barrel and tied her up to rest a little before beginning on the grass. He got upon Nellie and rode away to see how far it is to Cordes, for we must soon have more water.

## Sunday, September 4

Fred came back to camp with the report that Cordes Station was about five miles away. He had not gone clear to it. This morning we started very early without even eating our breakfast, except an apple apiece to stay our appetites.

At about eight o'clock we got to Cordes Station which consists of several houses, a store and post office. Several signs such as "70 mi. to Greene the Hatter's," "To the Bee-Hive," etc., upon the sides of barns made us feel near Phoenix. We watered the horses and filled our canteen at the well and then drove out about one-fourth mile till we came to a little grass.

We camped here and stayed till about two o'clock. We cooked and ate breakfast—a fashionable nine o'clock breakfast, and crawled under the shade of the wagon to read until one o'clock. Then we cooked the hard-shelled squash and ate dinner. The squash tasted very good. It was ten miles to Bumble Bee. The road was quite hilly in some places,

Cordes, 1902. *Arizona Historical Society/Pioneer Museum, Flagstaff. NAPHS #32-1169.*

but there was a long, level stretch through a vale which we much appreciated.

We got down Antelope Hill all right and reached Bumble Bee about six o'clock. It is a town of a few buildings and one family, which we call Mr. and Mrs. Bumble Bee and the little Bumble Bees. We camped near the house, and, judging from the loud squalling we heard during the evening, Mrs. Bumble Bee must have been stinging some of her little ones.

The Bradshaw Mountains lay to the west and the sun hid behind their tallest peak at six o'clock, an hour earlier than the usual sunset.

## Monday, September 5

This morning Fred mended the wagon brake for Black Canyon Hill. We started about eight o'clock. The road was very mountainous all day, the roughest road we have traveled yet. Winifred and I challenged each other to walk to the Agua Fria River (ten miles). I think it was more comfortable to walk than to ride. A great part of the road had been blasted out of the mountains, leaving great jagged rocks sticking up.

Black Canyon Hill was fully as steep and long as we had expected, and we were thankful that we were coming down and not going up. We pedestrians kept up pretty well until we were within two miles of the river. Then we began to prolong our rests and to increase their frequency until I yielded to Fred's invitation to get in and ride the rest of the way.

But Winifred could not be prevailed upon to change her purpose and [she] walked on to the river, where we are at this writing.

A Mr. McFee lives here. We are camped near his house under the scanty shade of a mesquite tree and a broiling midday sun. Arthur unharnessed the horses, Fred built a fire, I stirred up a pan of camp bread, and Winifred was tired enough to do the rest-(ing). In fact, we were all tired and hot. So when Fred returned from Mr. McFee's with the news that he had invited us to sit in the shade between his two houses, we went straightaway.

Mr. McFee's odd manner of speech and the queer things he said quite amused us. Fred had told him that we were hastening to Phoenix for school. We greased the wagon at this camp and it made Sister and me very sorry to think that it was probably the last time we should ever help lift the dear old wagon.

At four o'clock we were on the road again, hoping to reach New River by evening, a distance of twelve miles. But the road was still very hilly, and although we lightened the load by walking most of the way, Victoria got the droops again and we had to stop and make a dry camp. Vic got the two buckets of water in the barrel because she was sick, you see, but poor Nellie got none.

We had eaten supper on the road, so all we had to do was to spread out our beds on the hillside and go to sleep. The first was easily and quickly done, but alas! Either on account of the mosquitoes or the fruit we had eaten for supper, or both, or something else, we *could not* go to sleep, not one of us until about midnight.

We rose at five o'clock and started before daylight. It was about three miles to the first water on New River, at Alkire's Ranch. Winifred, Arthur and I walked to it and got there just as the sun was peeping over the eastern mountains.

We stopped at the ranch to water the horses and ate our breakfast in the wagon. A white-haired old gentleman (father of the Alkire Brothers of Phoenix) sold us some hay and told us it was an exceptionally cool morning, didn't we think

Alkire Place, New River, 1902. *Arizona Historical Society/Pioneer Museum, Flagstaff. NAPHS #32- 1159. (George Hochderffer Collection)*

so? But we didn't. We were now forty miles from home.

Between this ranch and the next, a distance of three miles, there were very few hills. The man at the second ranch said we could get water seven miles further on. So we didn't fill the barrel there as we had intended. But we drove and drove and drove and drove without a sign of water. At last a stage passed us and the driver told us that Mud Tanks was at least seven miles farther on.

We had hoped to reach that beautiful spot before our midday stoppage, but poor Vic's staggers attacked her again so we had to stop on the desert. There was some fine-looking range grass scattered about in patches which we thought would be fine for the horses. But before they had grazed long on it we noticed their mouths bleeding. Evidently the grass was cutting them, so Fred had to break out his baled hay.

Today we have come into the region of the tall cacti, which have a very familiar and home-like look to us. We hardly knew what to do to pass away the time till five o'clock, the time we had set to start again. The sun was very warm, so we kept close to the wagon for shade. Winifred spent part of the time giving Fred a shave so that he might be recognizable to the home folks.

At five o'clock we started, and [we] reached Rain Tanks, a muddy pool on the desert, at sundown. Our canteen was empty, and of course we were all very thirsty. So after we had watered the horses we built a little fire and boiled a canteen-full of water. We couldn't wait for it to cool in the canteen, so we poured a little into plates and drank it greedily. We decided that there would surely be nothing like water to quench a person's thirst.

We then drove on, hoping to make the Arizona Canal before stopping. But we found at ten o'clock that we couldn't do it on account of the horses, so we stopped.

Winifred and I had been walking to lessen the load and had heard two rattlesnakes singing their hideous songs close by the road. This made us rather afraid to spread our pallets on the bare ground, but as we knew of no other place nearby that would better serve the purpose, we were forced to overcome our fears and lie down on the sand among the cacti and greasewood. We thought that by rising with the moon at midnight we might still reach Phoenix in time for our little surprise. Arthur was so afraid we would not wake soon enough that he refused to sleep on his pallet. He lay down on the wagon seat instead, that he might wake us at the appointed time. His watchfulness seemed a hindrance to our slumbers, however, for about every fifteen minutes (at least so it seemed to me) he would raise up and ask Fred if it wasn't time to hitch up. Though we got no sleep, we were rested and Arthur finally persuaded us to get up. We dressed dreamily in the moonlight and at one o'clock were going towards home. We sang and talked at first to keep awake, but [we] gradually lapsed into silence. Soon Winifred might have been asleep in the back end of the wagon and Arthur [was] stretched across the back seat. Fred and I took turns driving and napping.

When we got to the canal Fred watered the team. The passengers also awoke and condescended to drink a little of the muddy water.

The Phoenix Mountains and "Old Camel's Back" now looked quite near. At last, as the eastern sky was lighting up and the chickens had begun their morning calls at the ranches, we turned into Grand Avenue. Then indeed we felt at home as we passed the familiar farms and houses. By this time Vic was pretty well tired out and Nellie was pulling her and the wagon, too. No amount of whipping could have induced Vic to quicken her pace, so Fred in despair took the iron poker and urged her gently along into town.

We were afraid we would be too late to wake the folks, for it was now quite light. As we neared the house, however, we noticed that there was no smoke rising from the chimney, so the folks were probably still abed. We left the team and wagon standing on the commons several rods away from the house so that they would not betray our approach.

We thought there would be no trouble in getting Vic to stand there since she had been so unwilling to travel. But as we left her she started to follow, as much as to say that she too was glad to get home. Fred fastened the brake tight to keep her back and we hurried on, on tiptoes.

We entered the front gate and tried the parlor door. But it was locked, as we had expected. So we walked softly around the house and, standing at the corner of the summer bedroom, began to sing "Home, Sweet Home." Of course our voices trembled some, and Arthur was seized with a fit of laughter so that the bass was lacking. But what did it matter if the tune were not rendered perfectly? It was the sentiment of it that we wished to emphasize.

In a moment a little brown-haired girl in a night dress was at the screen beaming with smiles but too confused and startled to know just what to say. Then came Father, dear gentle Father, declaring that it was the sweetest music he had ever heard.

How pleasant it is to get home when people are so glad to see you! We quite agreed with "Farmer John" that the best of a journey is getting home. And now my journal is ended, and I need only to add that the last seven weeks have been full of the most unalloyed happiness for me that I have ever had. School begins next Monday and I am sure we can all start into work with more energy for having taken our mountain trip.

Adios,
Zella Dysart

# Suggested Reading

Babbitt, James E. "Trading Posts along the Little Colorado River." In *Historic Trading Posts, Plateau Magazine of the Museum of Northern Arizona* 57 (1986): 2-9.

Barnes, Will C. *Arizona Place Names.* University of Arizona General Bulletin No. 2 (January 1935). Tucson, Arizona: University of Arizona.

Bass, William Wallace. *Adventures in the Canyons of the Colorado.* Grand Canyon, Arizona: By the author, 1920.

Corle, Edwin. *The Story of the Grand Canyon.* New York: Duell, Sloan and Pearce, 1946.

Hochderffer, George. *Flagstaff Whoa! The Autobiography of a Western Pioneer.* Flagstaff, Arizona: Museum of Northern Arizona, 1965.

Hughes, J. Donald. *In the House of Stone and Light.* Grand Canyon, Arizona: Grand Canyon Natural History Association, c. 1978.

James, George Wharton. *In and around the Grand Canyon.* Boston: Little, Brown and Co., 1911.

_____. *The Grand Canyon of Arizona: How to See It.* Boston: Little, Brown and Co., 1918.

Lockwood, Frank C. *More Arizona Characters.* University of Arizona General Bulletin No. 6 (July 1942). Tucson, Arizona: University of Arizona.

Lummis, C.F. *A Tramp Across the Continent.* New York: Charles Scribner's Sons, 1909.

Madsen, Lisa D. "The Grand Canyon Tourist Business of William Wallace Bass: The Early Years, 1885-1901." Paper delivered at the Arizona Historical Society Convention, Scottsdale, Arizona, 1 May 1981.

Maurer, Stephen G., ed. *Grand Canyon by Stage.* Albuquerque, New Mexico: Century Co., 1925.

Page, Susanne and Jake. *Hopi.* New York: Harry N. Abrams, Inc., 1982.

Sutphen, Debra. "Too Hard a Nut to Crack:" Peter D. Berry and the Battle for Free Enterprise at the Grand Canyon, 1890-1914, *Journal of Arizona History* 32 (Summer): 153-172.

Van Dyke, John C. *The Grand Canyon of the Colorado.* New York: Charles Scribner's Sons, 1920.

Wahman, Russell, "Grand Canyon Stage Line," *Desert Magazine* (January 1974): 32-35.

Waters, Frank. *Book of the Hopi.* New York: Ballantine Books, 1963.

Woods, G.K., comp. *Personal Impressions of the Grand Canon of the Colorado River near Flagstaff, Arizona . . .* San Francisco: The Whitaker and Ray Co., 1899.